THE
10
TOUGHEST
SALES
CALLS

To Kathryn,

Words could never express the amount of appreciation and debt of gratitude you are owed. The only utterance I can think of is: thanks!

Special thanks to:

> Steve Keats
> Gail Macmillan
> Les Withey
> Henny TenWolde
> Dr Karen Philips
> Chuck Nolton
> Doug MacMillan

Collectively, you have not only inspired and corrected; you were also brutally honest when you needed to be. I forgive you anyway.

THE 10 TOUGHEST SALES CALLS

AND HOW TO CLOSE THEM!

John MacMillan

KOGAN
PAGE

First published in 1994

Kogan Page Limited
120 Pentonville Road
London N1 9JN

© John MacMillan, 1994.

British Library Cataloguing in Publication Data

A CIP record for this book is available from the British Library.

ISBN 0 7494 1278 X

Typeset by Photoprint, Torquay, Devon
Printed in England by Clays Ltd, St Ives plc

Contents

About the Author

John MacMillan is one of those rare salespeople whose professional experience spans the globe. In his 25 years' experience of selling he has lived and/or worked in over 40 countries including various parts of the USA, Canada, the West Indies and Central America and most European countries, including the UK. During this time he has directed sales forces in a dozen markedly different cultures and closed over 10,000 pieces of business.

Drawing on this vast wealth of experience, John MacMillan has written a sales manual with a difference. Whatever stage you have reached in your sales career, *The 10 Toughest Sales Calls* cannot fail to help it on its way.

John MacMillan now lives in the French West Indies.

Introduction

As the title of this book suggests, we will examine the ten toughest sales calls you are likely to come across in your day-to-day selling – and close them! No, this is not an idle promise, it is a fact. You can and will dramatically improve your closing percentage. Effective selling is to a large degree a simple matter of common sense and hard work combined with a systematic approach to long established *basic rules*.

Selling, after all, is the oldest profession in the world. Really! Think about it: any product or service must be sold before it is rendered. In fact, nothing happens in any business environment until somebody sells something to someone. For this reason, a career in sales logically positions you in the hub of all commercial activity. Selling is where the action is!

There are many types of selling to choose from: retail, delivery, technical, product, service or order-taking. What this book will concentrate on is how to become the order-getter. This is 'real' selling and epitomizes creative sales. Creative sales is the ability to resolve a customer's problem and secure an order when other salespeople could neither resolve it, nor perhaps even see it. The challenge is to perform what others will not, or cannot do. 'Some men succeed because they are destined to, but most men succeed because they are determined to.' (anonymous)

Order-getters are not only determined, they also have many other attributes, among which are desire, conviction and motivation. An order-getter succeeds because he or she is not afraid of the hard work or the *constant practice of the fundamentals in the sales profession*. With this theme in mind, I came to create a fictional salesperson named Jack Average who is the central character in Part 1.

Jack was once a sales star. His talent however was quickly fading and taking his career with it. He had become a salesperson on his 'way out' due to boredom, complacency and lack of motivation. By going back to the basics, Jack methodically brings his slide to an abrupt halt and begins to re-discover his true potential. In the first half of the book we will follow Jack's metamorphosis through his odyssey in the ten toughest sales calls.

Jack's character was inspired by my own first mentor, years ago. This individual, although abundantly gifted with sales ability, wasted away into sales oblivion. I look back with a great deal of melancholy thinking about the accomplishments that could have been *but never were*. I rue the period because I was powerless to prevent it at that stage of my development. As my own career evolved I became convinced that this episode didn't have to occur; it could have been prevented. Part 1 explains, for the novice and veteran alike, how to get on track and stay on track.

When I had outlined a list of the 'nastiest of the nasty sales calls', choosing ten was painful, especially when factoring into the equation the ways in which two individual personalities can interact. This one complexity alone can make a simple sales call for one individual become a nightmare for someone else. After what seemed like an eternity of picking, choosing, changing and choosing again, I believe we have emerged with ten solid case studies to examine. These cases will provide you with a basis for closing not only these calls, but *any call*.

I hasten to point out that the approaches that I have used in these illustrations *are not* the only methods available. There are hundreds of variations that could, or would work under slightly different circumstances within the framework of the case itself. The techniques that I have employed are meant to tackle the basic problem and, in general terms, illustrate the way to achieve your objective. Only *you*, however, can judge how much of any particular ingredient is needed so that the stew tastes right to you.

Part 2 of the book deals with the basics of our chosen field – the building blocks of our sales foundation. You may find that some chapters in the *Back to Basics* section deal with fairly elementary subjects. I hope you won't feel that they lessen the impact of the sales message: they shouldn't. These topics are incorporated to ensure that every aspect of the discipline is covered – virtually from A-Z. I would urge you not to skip the fundamentals; these establish the route to closing business. Being able to pound nails in a cabinet doesn't make you a cabinet maker. Being able to measure, cut, sand, plane, hammer and finish *does*!

Before we begin I would strongly encourage you to put yourself in the 'shoes' of our protagonist. Ask yourself what you would do in similar situations. If you have been involved in a particular case, how did you handle it? As you read each case, write down your ideas on alternate ways to tackle the problem. Involve yourself. To paraphrase an old proverb: Tell me, I listen; show me, I see; involve me, I learn.

Remember to be yourself. You are a unique individual. Your approaches to selling are, and should be, reflections of your own character. There is an old German motto that best typifies this: 'When wealth is lost, nothing is lost; when health is lost, something is lost; when character is lost, all is lost.'

Finally, you have undoubtedly heard a great many claims of 'iron-clad', 'no fail' pieces of advice in your time. Sometimes they work, sometimes they don't! Each case study and chapter that you are about to read will provide you with no nonsense advice about what should and should not be done in sales. At the end of this book, however, I will give you ten words, which, if followed, will absolutely, positively guarantee your total sales domination over your competitors. The best already know and adhere to this credo, and so will you.

Part 1   Case Studies

The 10 Toughest Sales Calls

Prologue

Jack Average Meets his Conscience

Jack Average sat in his car with his hands on the steering wheel and his head bowed. He lifted his eyes and stared blankly at the cold avenue. 'Boy, I sure blew that one.' he thought to himself, 'No, I didn't blow it . . . I nuked it!'

Jack had just finished his last sales call for the day and would remember this one for some time to come. Mr Jordan had asked him to leave. 'No,' Jack painfully reminisced, 'Jordan didn't ask me to leave, he threw me out.' Jack could recall having his rear end hauled over hot coals before, but nothing quite like this. Crawling into the woodwork would have been merciful. Instead he was forced to crawl out of Jordan's office without a hope of redemption.

Slowly, he pulled away from the curb. His mind was filled with serious doubts about his career. 'I really never wanted to be in sales in the first place' he thought. Somehow things were getting confused for Jack. It wasn't only the job. Everything in his life seemed to be coming apart.

It was only 4.15 pm and Jack knew that he should be returning to his office. He realized however that he couldn't face his co-workers today, and perhaps never could again. It was three months since Jack was told by his boss that he had better 'shape up' and start meeting his quotas . . . or else. It just wasn't happening. In fact, his performance was getting worse instead of better.

Jack exited the motorway and headed towards the coast a few miles away. He needed some time alone to think about things. Jeffrey, his brother, needed a delivery driver but Jack could not face that final humiliation. He had to come to grips with what he should do with his life. It seemed obvious to him that selling was not it, but neither was driving a delivery van.

He parked his car and thought that the weather was perfect for his frame of mind – heavy fog and damp. As he walked along the cliffs, scarcely aware of the thunderous waves crashing against the rocks below, he was startled by an old man who emerged from behind a wooden shelter 50 yards ahead. Jack instinctively turned and was heading back towards his car when he heard the old man call out an arresting word that seemed to describe his whole life, '*Quitter*'.

Jack could not take another step. He stood paralyzed on the edge of the precipice. He wanted to run but his feet would not co-operate. Slowly he turned to face this craggy fossil of a man. *Was* he a fossil or an oracle, Jack wondered? No one, except himself, knew that this one word aptly portrayed his entire existence up to now. Who else could possibly know his innermost secret? He himself rarely admitted it, even in his subconscious.

The old man approached him and Jack could swear that the intruder was actually floating, not walking! 'This is it Jack old man,' he muttered to himself, 'you've finally gone over the edge.' This wasn't funny in view of his present location. 'If this is what abject failure does to you, then you've actually hit bottom.' Jack was speaking aloud now. A compassionate smile illuminated the stranger's lined face as he said, 'Jack, you may be down but you are not out. You don't have to be a "failure" or a "quitter" unless you agree to be those things. You can succeed if you are determined to succeed.'

'Who are you? What are you? Where did you come from?' Jack stuttered. 'How do you know my name? How do you know anything about me?' The man stroked his grey beard thoughtfully and said, 'I am you! I am the inner voice and force that pulls each of us out of our depths of despair. I am the will-power that makes us go on. I am hope.'

Jack was momentarily stunned by these words; stunned, upset and confused. What did the old man mean? Inner voice. Inner force. Hope! None of this was making any sense. It seemed to him that he was having some kind of 'out of body' experience. Or maybe he had actually plummeted off the edge of the cliff and was talking to one of the angels. 'No,' he reassured himself, 'it's a trick of the fog or else it's a bad dream and in a minute I'm going to wake up.'

'You're not having a bad dream Jack, but I do agree that you must wake up,' the bearded stranger replied. Jack felt the urge to run but again could not. He was transfixed and had to hear more. He wasn't sure if this apparition was real or a very elaborate hallucination. Either way, he lacked the strength and the will to break away. It somehow didn't matter whether it was real or imaginary. Jack sensed that some of his self-torment would go away if he could only talk things out . . . even if it was with a figment of his imagination. After all, wasn't this what self-examination was all about?

'What should I call you?' Jack mockingly began. 'Help,' the old man smiled knowingly. 'You can call me Help, because that is what I will always be to you. I know everything about you Jack. I know about your sense of failure. I know about your sales career being in serious jeopardy. I even know why Mr Jordan demanded that you leave his office this afternoon.'

Jack decided to stop fighting at this point. There was no point in kidding himself or this . . . whatever he or it was. He needed all the help he could get and he knew it. 'All right,' Jack said, 'I don't know who or what you are, but let's get one thing straight; stop talking like you just came off the set of The Ten Commandments. It makes me feel like I should drop to my knees every time you open your mouth. Can't I call you Jimmy or Mo or Squiggy or something?'

'You can call me whatever makes you feel most comfortable Jack, but I'll always answer to Help.' Help then placed his hand on Jack's shoulder.

'You used to be a very good salesman, Jack. There was a time when you had a great deal of self-confidence but still had a sense of humility. Back then you didn't take your talents for granted and you applied 100 per cent of yourself to your career, your customers and to every sales call that you made. This was, in fact, the reason why you had self-confidence. You were working in harmony with your goals and you were working at being your best.

'What has happened to you now is not new. It has been repeated throughout the ages of men. You have allowed success to go to your head. When you place yourself on a pinnacle, you are setting yourself up for a fall. It's dangerous enough when others flatter you to those heights but even then we should never be lulled into a belief that we cannot fail. Flattery may be heaped upon your dinner plate; however, it should be ingested in only very small quantities.'

Jack winced at this monologue. He recognized himself immediately in the images that these words conjured up. As much as he hated to admit it, the scene that the old man described was exactly the point at which he and his career had begun to slide. If he was going to get back on track he needed Help and he knew it.

Help looked at him in a kindly manner. 'You have to get back to the basics Jack. Forget about your past successes for now. They will always be good re-enforcements later, after you have begun your ascent from the abyss that you currently find yourself in. Do you know why your last sales call today ended in total disaster? I'll tell you why. You broke one of the cardinal rules in selling. You lied to Mr Jordan.' Jack broke in defiantly, 'I didn't lie to him. I just said that our product would meet the specifications for his conveyor.'

The old man looked down and then slowly lifted his head. 'Jack, your situation will never be improved if you can't be honest with yourself. You and I and Mr Jordan all know the facts, don't we? Perhaps you would prefer to have me go over the details of your attempted ruse?' Jack could not bear it. There was no escape from the truth. 'No, I'll do it,' he answered. 'I knew that if he bought the interface that I was trying to sell him, he would, in effect, be buying a piece of equipment that is basically obsolete. It is going to be replaced by a far superior product that we have coming out in several months. The thing is, I figured that I could go back and sell him the upgrade in six months or so and get another commission. The problem, I discovered, was that he knew that we had the new version already with our production people and I suppose he felt that I shouldn't be trying to unload my old stock off on him.'

'Good,' the old man said. 'This is your first step towards regaining honesty and commitment towards your customers. These qualities are what made you the asset that you were to them in the past. You were once a problem solver and you will be again. You don't need cheap tricks to sell a worthwhile product. The single requirement is that you sell from your customer's point of view. This is what I meant by going back to the basics. Go home and read the diary that you kept when you began your sales career. Throughout your first five working years, you recorded the most important knowledge you were taught in basic selling. You learned then because you believed that you had something to learn. You stopped learning lately for the opposite reason. Read your diary tonight, then tomorrow you and I will begin closing The Ten Toughest Sales Calls.'

Seeing the Decision Maker

Jack woke up early feeling as if he had run a marathon. He was tired and momentarily confused. What was it that he had dreamed last night? Ah yes, something about himself and his flagging sales career. Now, he had to work out what it was that he was supposed to do about it. Jack reminisced, 'I thought I was going to quit today. Why is it that I somehow feel that I have to give this thing a few more days?'

Jack struggled with his foggy thoughts for several moments and failed to come up with the answer. 'This must be what people mean by sleeping on it,' he mused. Quickly, he got dressed and called his office to let his boss, Pat Gormley, know that he would be in his territory north of the city, until the weekend. 'I'll see you Monday morning Pat. I think that you and I have a few things to talk about.' Pat tried to find out what he meant, but he was cut short by Jack's 'cheerio'.

Jack went into the kitchen to get his car keys off the table and saw a book lying beside them. It was an old diary he used to keep when he first got into sales. He scratched his head and tried to remember how it got there. He didn't remember that old thing for years. In his car, driving north, Jack continued to be plagued with nagging thoughts about his dream last night. It seemed so real, but he could barely remember what it was about. One thing for sure, the book in his case was real. Suddenly, an inner voice asked, *'Jack, are you prepared for your visit with Mr McIntyre? What is your objective for this call? Is McIntyre the decision maker?*

Jack was startled by the clarity of these questions. He thought for a moment, then answered each of them honestly: 'No; I'm not sure; I don't think so.' Pulling into a lay-by, he telephoned Mr McIntyre with the request that he see him an hour later than scheduled. McIntyre had no objection, so Jack sat down and reviewed all of his records on this account. He saw that although they were a regular buyer, they never really made any major purchases from his company. In fact, they were a 'class D' customer for him, yet their volume potential was 'VIP'.

Delving further into his files he began to realize that the only orders that he ever sold were under £1000! Could it be that McIntyre had authorization to purchase only up to this limit? Yes, that must be it. It was the only logical explanation in view of the fact that he had lost sales in the past when he had both a superior product and the best price.

He arrived at McIntyre's plant a few minutes early and decided to talk to the receptionist about her company. Jack discovered that his contact's boss was the financial comptroller. It was all beginning to make sense, McIntyre had to get approval from Margaret White before he could exceed his spending limit.

Jack entered the men's room, straightened his tie and combed his hair. He was going to look the part of the dynamic professional, even if he hadn't been feeling that way lately. When he returned to the lobby the receptionist informed that 'Mr McIntyre will see you now'.

As Jack approached McIntyre's office he was getting excited. 'Today, I'm going to get him. This will be the biggest order that we ever received from them. There is no way I'm letting him off the hook this time.' Jack was really psyched up.

Jack was met in the hall by McIntyre and escorted onto the firing line!

'Good morning Mr McIntyre, how is everything today?'

'Fine thanks. How about yourself?'

'Never been better, thank you.'

Jack looked around McIntyre's office and spotted a sports magazine on the credenza. For five minutes or so, they talked about the upcoming championship matches. McIntyre was really excited about his team's chances. Jack was pleased that his buyer was now suitably relaxed and ready for business.

'Well, Mr McIntyre, I suppose I'd better stop talking sports before I end up sidelining us both for the rest of the morning,' he chuckled.

'You're right, Jack. I can see that you're as bad as I am when it comes to talking about Manchester and Newcastle. The next time you're in we'll do a post match analysis.' McIntyre laughed aloud.

'Well, on to business.'

'Right you are. I came by this morning to see if you need a repeat order of widgets for the plant right now, Mr McIntyre?'

'Well yes, I believe we will be just about out by the end of the month. How about sending me 500 of the usual type next week?'

'No problem,' Jack said, and he began to write up the order. 'Mr McIntyre, I've been meaning to ask you about your conveyor system. The last time you and I were talking, you mentioned that your company may be looking to replace your current machinery because your production rate is falling behind your competitor's. I believe you said that if you don't do it soon, your higher costs may make your products less competitive in the market place. Do you still intend to make the change?'

'Well actually, Jack, we're still looking into it.'

Jack began to panic. He knew that they must be getting close to making a decision. At the very least they had probably already short-listed two or three suppliers for the job and he was yet to make a bid. Here he was, Jack the superstar, wanting desperately to land a big fish, and he didn't even have a rod. In fact it looked as if he'd have as much chance of landing this fish as he would of pulling a piranha out of the Amazon with his bare hands. Jack's mind was racing over the possibilities of what he should do next when . . . *'Calm down Jack. You need not fail. Use tact and diplomacy. Ask him if major purchases are generally decided by two or more people.'*

'Who the hell is that?' he asked himself.

'Later, just ask him,' came the reply.

'Mr McIntyre,' Jack said aloud. 'Is your organization like many others where major purchases are generally decided by two or more people?'

'That's good Jack. You gave him a graceful way out. No one likes to admit that they don't have the power that they pretend to have.'

'Yes, actually, they frequently are. Mrs White, our comptroller, usually gets involved.'

'I know this is short notice, but is there any chance that we can get together with Mrs White this morning?'

'Well, let me see if she is available.'

McIntyre left his office for a few minutes and returned with Margaret White. Jack reached into the breast pocket of his jacket and produced a business card which he handed to her. When White looked at it, it was printed right side up. She seemed impressed with this first impression. Jack was pretty proud of himself and this manoeuvre. It appeared that he was off to a good start. Following the introductions, Jack began his presentation from the beginning. He knew exactly how to proceed.

White was the new team member who had to be sold. Although McIntyre was already in Jack's corner, he would be careful not to ignore him during their discussion. Jack began by asking what criteria they used in selecting equipment and a supplier. He decided to use the 'Customer Benefit' presentation and ensure that the six key points (awareness, interest, evaluation, trial, decision and confirmation) were covered in sequence.

One hour later

'You've done an excellent job with your presentation young man.' Mrs White seemed pleased. 'Mr McIntyre, here, has told me many good things about your company. I understand that we currently carry many of your parts, but not much in the way of machinery. Perhaps we should change this.'

'Thank you very much.' Jack was beaming.

Jack thought, 'now I'll tell her about other customers who have bought the same type of machinery and how they are getting along with it. That will really impress her!'

'*Jack. Stop right there.*' There was that voice again. Jack was both angry and worried. Was he losing his mind? What was the problem now?

'*Jack. You've got your buying signal. It's time to stop talking about your product and close the sale. Recap your points, get their agreement and have them sign the order. I'll talk to you later when we're alone.*' Jack was certain that he really was going crazy.

'Mrs White, Mr McIntyre, you agree then, that our machine will do the job for you?'

'Yes,' they both confirmed.

'Our price is within your budget?' Again, 'Yes.'

'Our delivery schedule meets your needs?'

'It certainly does. We can be up and running a full month earlier than we expected to be.'

'Does our maintenance programme comply with your company requirements?'

McIntyre turned to White. 'No problems there, so far as I can see.'

'Finally, does our full-year complete warranty put you both at ease about our standing behind our product?'

'You, your machine and your company are just what we need.'

'Thank you. May I write up the order?'

'Please do,' Mrs White said. 'It's a pleasure doing business with a professional.'

Once outside in the car, Jack wondered about the little voice that he had heard during the crucial parts of his presentation. 'I don't know who or what you are,' he murmured aloud, 'but thanks for the help when I needed it.'

'You're welcome,' came the reply.

Case 2

Budget Constraints

Jack was feeling good after his call with McIntyre and White. For the first time in his career he had actually found a way to see the decision maker without offending his normal contact. Fortunately, he believed that the people he usually visited were decision makers and he need not repeat this last episode very often. 'But why not,' he thought. 'That really wasn't too difficult.' Yes, he *would* do it again if necessary. In fact, he'd do it for each sales call where he wasn't 100 per cent certain that he was talking to the right individual.

On his way to see Lou Grover at Ritol, he replayed their last meeting over in his head. Lou was quite a challenge in many ways. It was never easy to get him on track, businesswise, because of his never-ending practical jokes. But difficult as it was to talk business with Lou, it was even more difficult to get him to buy anything. Lou just didn't like to spend money. As Jack recalled, Lou didn't think that Ritol could afford to change their heavy plant equipment this year. Dear Mr Grover constantly moaned, 'this hasn't been the greatest year for profits.' Jack thought about this. 'If someone is making less money, and is asked to spend more, how can they come out ahead?'

The more Jack thought about the dilemma, the less optimistic he was that there was a sale to be made at Ritol today. He'd need a lot of help on this one.

'*Hello, Jack.*'

'Is that you again?'

'*Yes it is. It appears that you have a real challenge ahead of you on this one.*'

'Look. After much thought I've more or less decided to accept your presence in my head. I'm probably going crazy, if I'm not already there, but I don't want you to interfere in my thought processes unless I ask for you. Just hang in there and surface when I need or want you.'

'*As you wish Jack.*'

'OK. Now then, I can't work out what possible good I can do with Lou Grover on his much needed equipment.'

'*Why do you say "much needed"?*'

'Ritol has been putting off buying this equipment for over a year-and-a-half. Each time I ask Lou when he expects to take the plunge, he either makes a joke to avoid the issue or complains about his profits, or lack thereof.'

'*But why do you say "much needed"?*'

'Their plant is one of the oldest in their industry. The machinery they use has been around for so long that the Phoenicians were peddling them until they discovered that they were obsolete back then. Three major industrial advancements have passed them by in the last five years. Ritol's production is basically half of what it should be. It's half of what their competition is currently achieving.'

'*Is that costing them extra money in their production budget?*'

'It has to be. Between making half the product in double the amount of time, and in extra wages for all that manpower used on the job, their costs must be exorbitant.'

'*How much would you estimate their extra costs to be?*'

Jack thought about this for a minute. 'I'm not sure, but I intend to find out.'

When Jack arrived, Lou was down in the plant checking on yet another breakdown. Once again, Lou had on one of his weird and funky T-shirts:

WANTED

50 GIRLS FOR STRIPPING

MACHINE OPERATORS AT FACTORY

'How does this character get away with it,' Jack wondered. The last time Jack was in to see him, Lou was sporting a T-shirt that read: 'IVQII'. Jack smiled wryly. He remembered how Lou got him on that one.

'Go ahead Jack, what do you think it means?' Lou egged him on.

'I don't know Lou. Have you joined a Latin club or something?'

'Jack, old man, use your imagination.'

'I don't get it.' Jack was truly sorry. He wasn't so sorry for Lou, as he was for himself. Lou was fond of making him feel like a eunuch in a brothel when it came to his jokes. He made anyone and everyone feel like an absolute useless clod if they didn't get his punch-line the first time around.

'Go on, say it out loud,' Lou sniggered.

'All right, all right. Four queue two.'

'Again, but faster this time, and keep repeating it.' Lou was obviously enjoying this.

'Four queue two. Four queue two. Fork you too. Fork you too.' Lou was in stitches. 'Harharharhar. That's great Jack. We have to do this again some time. Harharhar.'

Jack recalled this episode with some amusement, but knew he had a job to do. He finally got Lou's attention and reminded him of their appointment.

'Jack, I'm sorry, I don't think I can see you today after all. I'm really very busy. These breakdowns are costing me a lot of time and money, and I can't afford either.'

'Lou, if you forgive me for saying so, I don't think you can afford not to see me today. These problems are not going away. If anything, you can expect them to get worse . . . much worse.'

'Look Jack, this isn't a good time. Can we make it next week?'

'No Lou. Please. I really think you should listen to me. I can solve these problems for you permanently, if you let me.'

'Have you brought some kind of black magic with you, or something.'

'Black magic – no; something – yes. I need about 30 minutes of your time. If you can spare me that, we can solve this headache forever.'

Back in Lou's office

Jack came in behind Lou, and was told to take a seat. As soon as he sat down the rudest noise emerged from the space between him and his chair. Phattttttttttttttttttt. Lou was in hysterics. 'What did you do Jack, sit on a duck?'

'That's good Lou,' Jack said with more than a slightly red face. 'The next time I'll stand if it's all the same to you.'

'Harharharhar. I've got something for that too,' Lou was still laughing uncontrollably. 'Listen Jack, seriously, before you begin I know what you're here for. You think that I need your new equipment. I need a lot of things. What I need most however, is money. I don't think that your company would be very pleased if you sold me products that I couldn't pay for.'

'Lou, for more than a year-and-a-half you have been in urgent need of a complete plant replacement. You haven't done it because of the expense. I think you're dealing in false economies that may eventually eat you out of house and home.' Jack sensed that he needed some shock treatment here. 'If you don't do something soon, you may not be here next year.'

'What exactly do you mean?' Lou was serious now.

'Lou, you are falling way behind the rest of the industry. Let's take a look at your current numbers. How many gizmos do you make in a day?'

'Seven thousand.'

'How many days are you working each week?'

'Seven. It's the only way to keep up with market demand – and our competition.'

'How many hours per day is your plant in operation?'

'Twelve.'

'How much does it cost you to make each gizmo?'

'Thirty-seven pence.'

'How much is labour costing you per hour?'

'Eighty pounds per hour with straight time, and £120 per hour on overtime.'

'Am I right in saying that you have eight hours of straight time Monday through Friday; four hours of overtime Monday through Friday; and the weekends are completely on overtime?'

'Yes, that sums it up.'

'All right, Lou, this is your overall picture.'

CURRENT PRODUCTION COSTS
7000 Gizmos/day
× 7 days/week
= 49,000/week
× 52 weeks
= 2,548,000/annum
× 0.37 cost/gizmo
= £942,760/annum

NON-OVERTIME LABOUR COSTS
8 hours/day @ £80/hour = 640 × 5 days
= 3200/week × 52 weeks
= £166,400/annum

OVERTIME LABOUR COSTS
4 hours/day (Mon–Fri)
= 20 hours
+ 24 hours (Sat–Sun)
= 44 hours @ £120/hour
= 5280/week × 52 weeks
= £274,560/annum

Now let's deduct labour costs to determine materials cost:

MATERIAL COSTS
£942,760 (total production costs)
− 166,400 (wages)
− 274,560 (O/T)

=£501,800/annum

'Our equipment has been proven to produce 1090 gizmos/hour. This would enable you to cut back to a nine hour day, and in only five days you could produce the same quantity that you currently produce. The system conversion cost for Ritol will be £625,000 after we take your trade-in. Now let's take a look at how the comparison stacks up:

PROPOSAL
1090 Gizmos/hour
× 9 hours/day
× 5 days/week

= 49,050/week
× 52 weeks

= 2,550,600/annum

NON-OVERTIME LABOUR
8 hours/day @ £80/hour
= 640/day @ 5 days
= 3200/week @ 52 weeks
= £166,400/annum

OVERTIME LABOUR
1 hour/day @ £120/hour
= 120/day @ 5 days
= 600/week @ 52 weeks
= £31,200/annum

MATERIAL
501,800/annum

TOTAL PRODUCTION
COSTS/ANNUM:

£501,800 (materials)
166,400 (labour-straight time)
31,200 (labour-overtime)

£699,400/annum
divided by 2,550,600 gizmos/annum
PRODUCTION COSTS: £0.2742/gizmo
(26 per cent less than current cost)

COST SAVINGS PER ANNUM
£942,760 (current production costs)
−699,400 (proposed production costs)

= £243,360 savings/annum

COST OF NEW EQUIPMENT: £625,000
divided by
SAVINGS PER ANNUM: £243,360

EQUIPMENT PAID THROUGH SAVINGS: 2.57 years

'Lou, you can see that in just over two-and-a-half years your new equipment will be fully paid for by your savings alone. Now, let's take a snapshot view of the asset and cost sides of your consolidated balance sheet for this part of your operation alone:

CURRENT EQUIPMENT

ASSET VALUE:	£100,000
DEPRECIATION:	20,000
PRODUCTION COST:	£942,760
LIABILITY:	£822,760

PROPOSED EQUIPMENT

ASSET VALUE:	£625,000
DEPRECIATION:	62,500
PRODUCTION COST:	£699,400
LIABILITY:	£136,900

This illustration clearly shows you that if you take this business unit in isolation your asset value goes through the roof and your liability drops through the floor.'

'I don't know, Jack. It appears quite attractive on the surface, but it still seems complicated to me. You make it sound that if I spend all this money the company will actually be in better shape. I'm not sure that I entirely understand this.'

'Lou, can we get your finance people in here to review the figures to see if they agree with the calculations? Also, I'd like a commitment from you that if they do agree, we can finally sign a deal.'

'Well I don't know. It's a lot of money.'

'Lou, you can't afford not to buy. Can I have your commitment and can we talk with your money people?'

'All right. Give me a few minutes.'

One hour later

'Well Mr Grover, I can't seem to find anything wrong with these calculations,' Beverly Smith the accountant was saying. 'I'd say that overall, this is a very good proposition.'

'Thanks, Bev, but don't forget we don't have the resources to spend this kind of money right now.'

'I realize things are tight Mr Grover; however, by saving almost ten pence per gizmo in production costs, we can increase our output to meet the strong market demand. A 26 per cent reduction in costs should give us a definite competitive edge.'

'I agree,' Jack said. 'Another area you should also look into, Lou, is the overtime cost associated with other departments which must work the same hours as your shift workers. For example, your distribution section has sorting, packing, order processing and deliveries based on your production schedule. These costs must be taken into account to get the total picture.'

'Mr Grover, the costs that Mr Average mentioned are running close to £100,000 per year,' Smith confirmed.

'That's it, Jack. You've won. Send me the contracts this week and let's plan to get the new system in here next month.'

'Thanks Lou, you won't regret this. Thank you Miss Smith for your invaluable input.'

As Jack was driving away he couldn't understand why he had never tried this approach before. He probably could have closed this sale a year or two ago. 'I suppose all I needed was a little Help to make me think of taking a new approach.'

Case 3

Exclusive Buying from a Friend

The hotel room was a mess. Papers and files were strewn everywhere. Jack was sitting cross-legged on the bed with a very perplexed look on his face. Since the Jordan call earlier this week, he felt that other things were beginning to go his way. First he got White and McIntyre to sign an equipment contract, and then this afternoon, he finally landed the 'big fish', Lou Grover. Now, what was he going to do about Fred Herbert tomorrow? He had been calling in to see Fred at ACME, on and off, for three years and had yet to be rewarded for his efforts. Fred only bought from Jack's competitor, Bob Cranshaw. The reason, Fred explained, was quite simple: Fred and Bob went to college together, and as Fred was fond of saying: 'What are friends for?'

Jack stared at the ceiling and wondered how he was going to break in on this account. There was nothing in the file that he considered helpful. He could neither find a clue, nor discover an angle. Jack thought, 'Maybe I could kidnap his first-born. No, I'd never get away with it,' he reasoned. He sensed that this would, most likely, be a total waste of time. He suddenly remembered that he seemed to get help by thinking that he needed some.

'What's the problem Jack? Are you considering giving up on Fred?'

'Hello again. It's good of you to drop by. How do you know when to come?'

'That isn't a major concern right now. What is a major concern however is what you are going to do tomorrow about Fred Herbert.'

'I give up. Ah, no, I mean I'm not sure. Do you have any suggestions on how to break "friendship" buying habits?'

'To begin with, Jack, find out how often Fred's friend visits him. Ask him if Bob Cranshaw's products are up to standards for Fred's plant manager. Does Bob keep him informed on product advancements? For example, your new relay switch is the best in your industry. Do you think that Bob told him about it? Try to sell Fred on its value. Convince him that Bob can't match it with anything that he offers. Finally, don't you think that you can persuade Fred that it's prudent to have a back-up supplier?'

'That's not a bad idea. I haven't tried that approach before. Fred, prepare for a new battle.'

'Never mind that. What you have to do is prepare your presentation for tomorrow and then get some rest.'

The following day at 8.30 am, Jack was sitting in Fred's office. Fred was shuffling papers around on his desk, and when he stopped, he began positioning some paperweights.

'Jack, if ever you wanted to read body signals, this is a classic case.'

'I think I know what you mean, Help. He has barely looked at me since I came into his office. Don't tell me . . . he's disinterested.'

'Yes, I think that's a fair assumption. What are you going to do about it?'

'It's time to get Fred fired up.' Aloud Jack said 'Fred. The reason why I came in to see you this morning was to talk to you about a new relay that we've just brought out.'

'Jack, you know that I buy all my stocks from Bob Cranshaw's company. They have been very good to me over the years.'

'Yes, I remember you telling me that. You know, Fred, from time to time I ask myself if you are getting the best possible service that you deserve.'

'Jack, be careful. This is delicate ground. If you attack his friend, directly or even indirectly, you ultimately attack Fred with your assault.'

'What I mean is, I concede the point that Bob is a great guy and his company makes good and reliable products. I wonder, however, if you are being kept up to date on product advancements in the industry – advancements that you should know about.'

'Yes, of course Bob keeps me updated. His company sends me regular flyers on anything new coming onto the market.'

'Fred, did you know about *our* new relay?'

'Well, ah . . . no.'

'You see, that's my point. My company has been written up in *Hi-tech* magazine about this breakthrough and it appears that Bob's company didn't tell you about it. Why should they? It would take business away from them.'

'Slow down Jack. Look at the signals that he is transmitting to you. They are as bright as a beacon: he's crossed his arms, his lips are pursed and his fists are clenched.'

'Wow, you're right. I almost forgot to keep checking on his body language. He sure looks wild. What do I do now?'

'Bring your presentation to a full stop. Find out why he is so upset.'

'I'm sorry if I've upset you, Fred. It's just that I'm only human. I get very frustrated when I know for sure that I can offer something far better than the next bloke and yet still can't get a piece of the business.'

'Jack, I don't appreciate your approach or style. I've told you already that I'm quite happy where I am.'

'Fred, may I ask you a few questions? I know that I'm not going to get any business today, but, with your permission, I'd like to keep visiting you. I think that maybe down the road, I'll be able to convince you that my company and I aren't that bad. We know Bob is good, but so are we.'

'No, I don't mind seeing you Jack; it's just that I don't like to be pressured.'

'I understand . . . no more pressure. Let me ask you something. Your honest answer would mean a great deal to me. My company is keenly interested in having you for a customer. Is it me you object to dealing with? If so, I could arrange to have someone else call on you.'

'For heaven's sake, no. I like you, Jack.'

'Is it my company you don't like?'

'Again, no. In fact your company is one of the most respected in the industry.'

'Then, it must be our product line.'

'No, your products are very competitive.'

'Our prices are out of line?'

'No. Your prices are also competitive.'

'Find out about how often he sees Bob.'

'Is it because you don't see me often enough?'

'That's not it, at all. In fact I think that I see you more often than . . .'

'Good Jack, you have him thinking.'

'Then, Fred, please tell me what it is that I'm doing wrong. I'll never improve if I don't know what needs correcting.' Jack was using the 'no sale today' close. He also thought about some other ways of getting around exclusive buying: selling divisions indirectly, executive selling and making Fred aware that he may not be keeping up with *his own* competition. Instead Jack felt that he should continue with his present tack.

'Jack, there is absolutely nothing wrong with you, your company or your products. I'm simply in the habit of dealing with the other people.'

'I understand about friendships, Fred. The world would be a sorry place if we couldn't count on our friends. The thing is, that in business, we are counted on by a lot of other friends – our co-workers. If we aren't keeping up with improvements in technology, I think that basically we must be falling behind the rest of the field. When we fall behind on a competitive level, sales suffer. When sales suffer, so do the employees and their families. What I'm trying to say is that it may pay to hedge your bets. I believe that competition keeps everyone sharp. In fact, competition is what has made the industrialized world what it is today. By dealing with only one supplier you, your co-workers and your company may ultimately suffer.'

Fred put his pen down, sat back for a minute, and said nothing. Jack's words had struck a chord in his mind. Maybe, just maybe, it made sense to have a back-up supplier. 'Jack, you've got a point. In fact, my plant manager was asking me about one of your products that he read about last week. Maybe it's this relay that you just described to me. I'll tell you what, send me four so that we can test them. If they work out well, I'll order replacements for all of our equipment.'

'I can't thank you enough Fred; you'll not regret this. Not only will you get the finest product on the market, I also promise to keep you updated on anything new that comes along. I'll always try to be one of your best business friends!'

Case 4

The Irrefutable Objection

Jack was whistling to the music on the radio as he drove along the motorway. 'This is great,' he thought. 'I really seem to be getting my old form back. I was pretty good with Fred this morning. No, I wasn't pretty good, I was damn good!' Jack hadn't felt so happy about his sales performance in years.

'Jack, you're not being overcome by your successes, I hope.'

'Ah, come on. Don't rain on my parade. In the last couple of days I have closed some pretty tough sales. It appears to me like I'm back in the fast lane.'

'Haven't you learned anything from the past? Think back to the time when you were in the "fast lane". What transpired in those "good old days" to de-rail your rapid ascent up the road of success? Wasn't it false pride and a belief that you could not fail? Jack, if you refuse to learn from your mistakes of the past, you are doomed to repeat them.'

'Yes, yes. You've made your point. Anyway, right now I have to concentrate on my next appointment. I'll be seeing Bill Walters of NORTEC in 30 minutes and I should be preparing for our meeting.'

Bill was eagerly awaiting Jack's visit. Half of his assembly line was shut down as a result of a faulty printed circuit board. If he didn't get it up and running within a day, or two at most, his company would have to default on a major contract they were working on.

As Jack strode into Bill's office, Bill virtually leaped out of his chair to greet him at the door. Jack had never seen this customer look so excited. 'Wow,' Jack was thinking, 'it must be my after shave.' Bill grabbed and shook his hand vigorously, then pulled him over to some drawings on his desk.

'Jack, my boy, am I happy to see you!'

'Bill, it's good seeing you again. Have I come at a good time?'

'You certainly have. Fully half of my production line is down due to a fault in the system. I think it may be a PC board. Do you have a few minutes to take a look?'

'Of course, lead the way.'

Once in the plant, Jack, Bill and the foreman spent the better part of an hour going over every circuit in the section containing the faulty part. Jack retrieved some electronic testing equipment from his car and was able to confirm that the problem was indeed a PC board, as Bill had suggested.

Jack was a little perplexed when they got back to Bill's office. He knew exactly what part was needed, but he was also aware that his company no longer stocked it. He might be able to find one in someone else's inventory, but felt it unlikely.

'So Jack, what do you think?'

'It doesn't look good, Bill. That PC board is a rather old version, and I'm not sure that I can find you the exact same part. I can check around at some of our other locations, but that's a long shot and it's going to take some time.'

'That's the problem, Jack. I don't have time. If I don't get us up and running within 48 hours we are going to forfeit the contract that we are working on.'

'I can still check if you want me to.'

'No it's OK Jack. I can get a substitute part from Base Electronics, that should allow us to get by. I really appreciate your help though.'

Jack pondered, 'I don't want to lose this order. Maybe I can sell him on a substitute part?'

'Listen Bill. I can supply you with a different model PC board. You know, it's our emergency "generic" board that basically fits all of these machines.'

'Yes, I thought about that. The only problem there is that it won't operate at the higher resolutions on our equipment which will slow us down considerably. I must complete the current order that we have in-house by the end of the month. If I don't finish it, we lose it. I don't believe that your "generic" board can see us through this one.'

'The thing that you should keep in mind Bill, is the fact that I can get you this part here by tomorrow morning. At least you can be back in production by then, and who knows, maybe it has a higher tolerance than we think it has.'

'I can't take that chance. The Base part isn't exactly what we need for our system either, but it's a better bet.'

'Bill, what about . . .'

'Jack, I find it hard to believe that you are still trying to sell this gentleman something that you know won't work properly. The more you attempt to convince him of its value, the more you will lower the esteem he has for you. You and he are both aware that your product will not adequately perform to his requirements. The "generic" board has special merits, and under different circumstances it may well have been his best option. However, he must complete his order in a time frame that is not possible with the solution that you are proposing. Remember Jack,

problem solvers do not receive every order, but they do receive the majority of orders!'

'What is it Jack?'

'Well Bill, I just remembered something. I saw one of my customers last week whom, I recall, suggested that Total Electronics may have the exact board you need. Why don't you give Bob Cranshaw a call and see if they have the part in stock?'

'Jack, if you're right, you may have saved my life. I'll call him right now.'

After the telephone call

'That's it! Bob's office said that they have the part and that they can have it here by tomorrow morning. Jack, I can't thank you enough.'

'It's all right. I'm just happy that I could be of help.'

'No, I won't forget this. First you identified the problem and then you solved it for me. I'm just sorry that I can't give you the order, but there will be other days.'

'I appreciate it Bill. I really don't mind missing out on an order if I can be part of the solution to one of my customer's problems. There is a lot more to business than simply making a sale.'

'Jack you're so right. I just wish more people thought like you do. Come back and see me next month, I have some plans for a plant renovation that I'd like you to take a look at. Your suggestions and opinion would be greatly appreciated.'

'Sure thing, Bill, I'll see you then. In the meantime, good luck with the board.'

'Jack, before you drive away, take a look behind you. The carpark is full of cars belonging to people who work here. Each of them depends on their job to maintain the kind of life that they and their families enjoy. If their company succeeds, so do they. What you have done here today represents the "sowing of seed". Although you cannot reasonably expect immediate results when working the field, you may depend on good work being eventually rewarded with an equally good harvest.'

Case 5

Your Price is too High (but it isn't)

Jack was feeling proud of himself when he started out from Bill Walters'
parking lot. In fact, he thought he felt just as good as he would have had
he made the sale. He remembered from his early days of sales training
that one of his instructors repeatedly lectured his class on the need to
sell *only from the customer's point of view.* 'If he doesn't need it, don't
sell it,' old Mr Brown would say. Looking back, Jack could see that
Brown was absolutely right.

His next call however, was not one that Jack was looking forward to.
Mr Mitchell was a real 'head case'. This old bird would think that he was
paying too much for Windsor Castle if the Queen offered it to him in
exchange for his pipe. Jack smiled and thought to himself 'I don't think
that Mitchell has ever paid full price for anything in his life. If his IQ and
his knowledge of prices were at the same level, we'd have to water him
twice a day.'

*'Just a moment Jack. Aren't you over-simplifying the situation slightly?
Perhaps, you've never sold Mr Mitchell on value.'*

'What do you mean, "sold him on value"?'

'Value = Quality+Service+Price.'

'I'm not sure that I get your meaning.'

*'It's quite simple. If a salesperson is going to sell by overcoming the
basic price objection, he can only do so by helping his customer to see
the true value of his product. For example, if you sold a drum of formula
for growing hair to someone for £100, and that person turned around,
bottled it and sold it for £200, would you say that your buyer received
good value for his £100?*

'I suppose so.'

*'If you sold a machine for £1000 that would last five years, you
guaranteed it for five years and it would allow your customer to make
£5000 over the five years, would you say that he received his money's
worth?'*

'Yes. He'd have a 100 per cent return on his investment per year.'

*'That then is value. In most cases a customer doesn't realize the worth
of a product being offered to him because no one has bothered to
explain its value. The customer must be shown the benefits that he will
receive by buying what is being offered.'*

'Yes, I remember. You can best sell your customer on your product by translating its features into benefits.'

'That's correct Jack. Do you think you can do it?'

'Just watch!'

Mr Mitchell looked particularly grumpy, Jack thought, as he waited to be asked to be seated. Finally Mitchell snapped 'sit down'. Not wishing to antagonize the 'old geezer', Jack dropped into his chair instantaneously. This was going to be a real battle. In the mood he was in today, it didn't seem likely that Mr Congeniality would be interested in much more than ripping out Jack's heart and feeding it to his pet tarantula. 'Well,' Jack thought, 'let the show begin.'

'Mr Mitchell, it's good of you to see me on such short notice. I realize that you generally like two weeks to prepare for your meetings.'

'Are you trying to be funny or something, Average.'

'No sir, I just meant that you usually don't see me this quickly. I was of the impression that you prefer two weeks notice before scheduling an appointment.'

'Unless you stop talking nonsense and start talking business, this is going to be the shortest appointment on record for both of us.'

'Yes sir, I'm sorry. I'll get straight to the point. I wanted to follow up on our last meeting. Have you given any more thought to our control panel?'

'No, I haven't. Have you given any more thought to your outrageous price for your control panel?'

'Actually Mr Mitchell, that's why I wanted to talk to you. I don't think that I adequately explained everything to you the last time I saw you. Our control panel perhaps offers some features that you may not have been made aware of.'

'Rubbish. One control panel is as good as any other. A control panel "controls", plain and simple. Now unless you have something worthwhile hearing, I believe this meeting is over.'

'May I ask you a question Mr Mitchell?'

'What is it?'

'What exactly are you looking for in the new control panel that you intend to purchase?'

'I'm looking for something that works.'

'Well, yes I know. Could you elaborate on that?'

'Young man, I want a piece of machinery to replace the other piece of machinery that no longer functions properly.'

'If I may be so bold as to suggest, Mr Mitchell, I don't believe that you easily tolerate incompetence or breakdowns in your factory. Is that a fair assumption?'

'I think you know the answer to that question. I expect that both people and machinery should operate correctly. If they do not ... out they go.'

'That's exactly my meaning. How old is the control panel you intend to replace?'

'Two years, why?'

'How much did you pay for it when you bought it?'

'A great deal less than what you are asking for yours.'

'Yes, I know, but how much did it cost?'

'Two thousand seven hundred pounds.'

'How much have you spent on maintenance and repairs over the two years of usage?'

'Five to six hundred pounds.'

'Have you had breakdowns within this period?'

'Yes, two, and I was damned annoyed about them.'

'I grant you, Mr Mitchell, that our panel is £1000 more expensive than what you spent the last time; but if you add the £500 to £600 that you paid out on maintenance and repair to the cost of the old machine, the difference between what I am offering compared to what you received is only £400 to £500. Therefore ...'

'You see, you just proved it to yourself. Your machine is still more expensive, and it would most likely break down as often as the one I have.'

'If I could prove to you that this is not the case, would you confirm the order?'

'That's good Jack; the "What-If" close is well chosen here. Make certain that you are comparing apples with apples before you proceed.'

'I suppose so. Now, what do you mean?'

'All right, first of all, did your present control panel come with an interface?'

'No. I paid an extra £400 for that.'

'Did it come with free installation?'

'No. I had to hire an electrician to do it.'

'How much did that cost?'

'One hundred and fifty pounds.'

'When you experienced the two breakdowns, how long were you down for?'

'The first time only a day. The second, they couldn't get the part here for two days.'

'Did you send your workers home when this happened?'

'No, of course not. They work for me in good and bad times.'

'So, that means that you paid them for, basically, standing around.'

'Not really standing around. I had them doing other odd jobs.'

'None the less, they weren't producing what it was that they were being paid to produce.'

'No.'

'Well then, let me explain about our control panel. To begin with it comes with an interface already built in. Here you save £400. We install it free of charge; another £150 savings. We guarantee this piece of equipment for two years and you get free maintenance and repair for the entire period. There you save, let's say, £550. Finally, our guarantee includes a maximum of four hours to repair the equipment, or else we supply a substitute until we get it fixed properly. If you add up these costs, the other panel is actually £100 more than ours. Finally, and this is a very important point, you don't have the aggravation or expense of paying employees for performing non-essential duties.'

Mr Mitchell paused momentarily as he evaluated everything that Jack had just told him. Jack knew he had him. 'At any moment the old chap is going to stand up, slap me on the back and tell me that I did a great job. I'd better be careful now and not show too much excitement. Control yourself, Jackie-boy, and just let the order drop into your lap.' Just as Jack was in the process of slapping *himself* on the back, Mr Mitchell's jaw tightened, he clenched his fists and he gave Jack such a piercing stare that Jack was certain that he must be having a seizure.

Jack's thoughts were racing. 'What the hell is wrong? I did everything according to the book. Why is he looking at me like that? Why is he picking up that letter opener? I never even had a chance to say goodbye to my brother Jeff and his delivery service.'

'What the devil is wrong with you Average? What kind of salesman are you anyway? Maybe you should consider taking up a meaningful profession like counting tadpoles in the Florida Everglades.'

'Sir, I don't understand. What did I do?'

'It's what you didn't do. Why didn't you explain this to me before? Those factory breakdowns I had cost me a lot of money. If you had done your job properly in the past, I could have avoided a great deal of aggravation and expense. Get your order book out. I'll sign the order today and you can send me a new control panel next week.'

'Yes sir.' Jack was careful not to react to the verbal abuse. Besides, the old devil probably had a right to give him a kick in the pants for not selling up to his potential in the past. Jack certainly wasn't doing either he or his customers any favours by just showing up for work. He smiled, opened his order book and asked, 'what day would you like it delivered?'

The Group Presentation: 'Your Price is too High' (and it is)

What a week Jack was having! Some of his toughest customers were having their barriers crushed under the weight of the steamroller he was riding. 'Easy boy,' he found himself saying. 'This can come apart as fast as it came together. I'm getting a lot of help on these calls and if the help stops, so do I.'

Help quickly interrupted. *'Jack, you are thinking nonsense. You have always had the ability. What you lacked was perspective and focus.'*

'Maybe, you're right. On the other hand, I haven't sold this well in years. In fact, I'm not sure I was ever able to sell this well. I can't help believing that you are doing all the thinking and I'm doing all the talking. It doesn't speak well for my sales ability.'

'Again this is total nonsense. All I am doing is simply providing you with reminders of information that is already in your head. You could say I am bringing to the foreground that which is in the background. None of what I have said to you is new. You have known these things for quite some time. Unfortunately, most people consider lessons to be something to read about and then forget; Jack, never forget what you have learned. Instead, apply what you have learned and you will always find the help you need within yourself.'

Jack sat in his car for a minute pondering what seemed to him these mystical words. Was he good, or was he pretending to be good based on this voice that he kept hearing? He looked at his watch and sat upright. His meeting with the Board of Directors of Malbay was due to begin in five minutes. This was another one of those 'tough calls'. He knew that his quotation was higher than Cranshaw's, but what he didn't know was who he had to convince that his product was a better buy. 'Who is the ultimate decision maker in the group?'

Malbay was, potentially, the largest account Jack had in his territory. Four weeks ago they contacted various suppliers to obtain bids for equipping a new plant that they were opening. Jack's company was one of those contacted. He had a very good working relationship with the purchasing manager, Shelly Gomes, but Jack was told by Shelly that major purchases were approved by the Board. The product presentation would have to be given to them. *They* would need to be sold.

The boardroom looked ominous: mahogany panelling, 12 leather chairs and a beautifully finished, circular hardwood table. As Jack was escorted into the room he began to get nervous. He was reminded of something that Shelly had said to him: 'Jack, you can expect to field many questions, especially since your price is higher than everyone else's.'

'Good afternoon ladies and gentlemen,' Jack began.

'Good afternoon Mr Average,' an impeccably groomed, authoritative looking lady responded. 'Please sit down.'

'On behalf of Totronics, I would like to begin by thanking the Board for this opportunity to meet with you this afternoon. I have taken the liberty of preparing a copy of our proposal for each Board member, and I have also included in each packet technical literature on our products. As I am going through the points in our offer, please feel free to ask any questions.'

'That won't be necessary Mr Average. We wish to hold all questions until you have finished your presention.' This time an elderly bespectacled gentleman, off to Jack's right, was speaking.

'This is going to be rough,' Jack thought. 'I thought that the lady I initially talked to was the leader, but now I'm not sure. Round tables don't provide much of a clue. I don't know which one to focus my attention on.'

Jack, don't neglect anyone. As you present your summary, be sure to look at each of them.'

Thirty-five minutes later

'Well, ladies and gentlemen, that completes my presentation. Thank you.'

'Mr Average,' the lady was speaking once again, 'thank you for a comprehensive explanation of your proposal. Ladies and gentlemen, shall we begin our questions, in clockwise order, starting on Mr Average's left?'

'Mr Average, how would you say that your product differs from others which are available in the market?'

'It is very difficult to draw a comparison without knowing which particular product to compare against. Each product has its own special features.'

Jack, that's good. First, this will allow you to determine who you're competing against. Second, watch where eyes turn to get approval for divulging the information on which products they are interested in.'

Jack thought that he saw the individual who posed the original question look towards the gentleman wearing the navy tie.

'Would you be kind enough to describe the differences between your system and that of 'Total Electronics?' The lady was speaking again. The situation was becoming quite confused. Jack was uncertain if the authoritative looking lady, the man with the glasses or the man with the navy tie would ultimately turn out to be the group leader. This information was vital. Once the leader was identified, Jack could begin honing in on that person's 'hot spot'. He had to know what exactly they were buying, before he could sell it!

Jack decided to go through the process of elimination. He would assume that the lady was in charge and direct all of his questions to her. He must ask her questions relating to company values, opinions and requirements. The leader normally sets the tone for such policy statements. If she turned out *not* to be the leader, she would turn to whoever was.

'Before I answer that, may I ask something?'

'Of course.'

'What is it that you ultimately want to produce for your customers?'

'We produce quality products that create satisfied customers and induce repeat buying.'

'What single image does Malbay want best to illustrate to its customers?'

'Quality.' The lady was still fielding the questions.

'If you had a choice between producing at a lower cost, thereby making more profits, or producing at a higher cost to maintain quality, which would you choose?'

This time there was a pause. She looked at her notes and quickly glanced over at the man wearing glasses. The lady then looked up at Jack and asked.

'What is the relevance of your question Mr Average? We wish to produce at the lowest cost, create the highest profits for our company and maintain our quality standard.'

'Yes, I understand that. In today's market, however, competition is changing radically. There are competitors in *every* field that cut costs by cutting back on quality. In effect they are building down to a price, rather than up to a standard. These same competitors do sell clone-like products to many buyers where cost, or price, is more important than the quality of the item. That is the reason for my question.'

'I'll answer that Jane,' the man wearing the blue tie responded. 'Mr Average, you bring up a very salient point on the condition of business thinking today. It is one which we, collectively, have given a great deal of thought. Our company has been in business for 82 years and throughout this period we have witnessed an unparalleled change in corporate philosophy within our industry. Quality used to matter to everyone. However, as you mention, many companies are now more interested in their bottom line than in producing quality goods. We, at Malbay, have always accentuated our quality image and it has made us the industry leader. There can be no compromise on quality for either we or our customers.'

'Based on your "quality" position sir, may I ask what is the primary criteria that you use when selecting a supplier?'

'Quality products require quality components.'

'Thank you sir. Now I feel that I am able to draw accurate comparisons between my system and that of Total Electronics.'

During the next hour Jack elaborated on points where his system had superior industry ratings compared to those of Total. He emphasized his specifications which, again, were of a higher calibre overall. His system produced fewer rejected pieces, worked faster and had fewer instances of down time. His company offered a guarantee of four-hour repairs, and they had the largest parts inventory in the country.

'In summation, ladies and gentlemen, I realize that the equipment we are proposing to you is not the least expensive on the market. Over the course of its life however, the difference represents a few pounds per day; a thousandth of a pence per piece per day. Isn't this a small price to pay in order to be assured of the quality products that you insist on? Finally, I would like to thank you for a very uplifting meeting today. It's a rare pleasure when I come across a company, which like my own, is more concerned with quality than it is about cutting corners. Once again, thank you for your time.'

'We wait and see, now,' Jack was thinking after he left Malbay's building. 'If they are genuinely concerned about quality, I've got what they need. I know that I impressed them with my presentation. I only wish that it was me making all these right moves, and planning all these brilliant strategies. I wonder where I would be without Help?'

Case 7

Fighting Pay-offs

Of all the things that Jack detested in business, the acceptance of bribes was among the lowest dregs in the 'bottom of the barrel of dirty tricks'. His next call was in this category. Two months had elapsed since he had seen Ben Bender. On the last ocasion he had stormed out of Ben's office in disgust, after he was plainly told that if he wanted the order, Ben expected a commission. Ben even went so far as to suggest that Jack should give him a phony invoice where prices were inflated by the 10 per cent that Ben wanted to personally pocket.

He realized that if he was going to make any progress with this account, he was going to have to find a way of working around Ben. Somehow, he had to get Ben's boss in the meeting and have her take control of the buying decision. This wasn't going to be easy. Ben guarded his little 'nest-egg' fairly closely, and he didn't like anyone else's involvement in what he was doing.

Jack thought long and hard about this problem. He could find out if one of his executives knew one of Ben's executives. In this way he could explain the situation to his senior manager and have him make a call on his counterpart in Ben's company. Alternatively, Jack could arrange to get his direct superior, Pat Gormley involved. He was certain that if Pat were coming for a visit he could convince Ben to have his direct superior, Jessica Miles, join the meeting. There was, however, another way that Ben could be circumvented. Jack decided to try it before asking for his management's assistance.

Every Monday for the last two months, Jack had called Ben's office and asked to speak to him. Once the call was passed through Jack would immediately hang up. This past Monday however, Jack was finally rewarded for his perseverance. At long last he heard the four words that he had been waiting to hear. 'Ben is on holiday', the receptionist informed him. Immediately, Jack asked to speak with Mrs Miles.

'Good morning Mrs Miles, this is Jack Average from Totronics.'

'Good morning Jack, what can I do for you?'

'Well, Mrs Miles, I was originally calling for Ben Bender, however I understand that he is on holiday.'

'Yes, that's right. Ben will be away for three weeks. How can I help you?'

Jack had orchestrated this moment perfectly. Totronics had come out with a new bearing six weeks ago that was twice as good as anything on the market. It lasted twice as long and was the same price as the bearing Ben was using. The exception here, however, was that Jack was quite certain he would actually have a tremendous price advantage! At a management meeting, he relayed the information on this account and Pat Gormley agreed that Jack *could* offer an introductory 10 per cent discount. This, coupled with Ben's 'normal' commission, should give Jack a 20 per cent price advantage. With Ben away, this was the time to act.

'Mrs Miles, we have recently come out with a revolutionary bearing that is proven to have twice the normal life of the bearings you are currently buying.'

'That's very interesting Jack. Perhaps you should wait and talk to Ben when he returns.'

'Yes, I could of course, but as an introductory offer we are discounting our prices by 10 per cent. I'm afraid this offer is only good through the end of the month, and Ben will still be away. If you are able to spare me ten or fifteen minutes of your time, I believe that we could save you a great deal of money.'

'Ordinarily, Ben handles these kind of purchases.'

'I realize that, Mrs Miles, and I generally work with Ben on these types of things, but I hate to see you miss out on such an opportunity. I just need about ten minutes.'

'All right Jack. Why don't you come by later this afternoon; say about 4 pm.'

'That's great. By the way, would it be possible to have one of your engineers stop by so that he or she could take a look at our specs on this bearing? Our company is looking for as much input from our customers as possible.'

'Yes, I think that could be arranged.'

'Again, thank you Mrs Miles. I'll see you at 4 o'clock.'

Later on that afternoon

'Jack, this is Ron Silver, our chief engineer.'

'Good afternoon Mr Silver.'

'Hello Jack. I understand from Jessica that your company has manufactured a new bearing that you claim lasts twice as long as anything else in the market.'

'Yes, that's right. I really appreciate you taking a look at it because our team of engineers is canvassing for technical input on this product. We already have plans for a second series and intend to incorporate designs based on the market needs.'

'That's fine. Let's take a look at what you've got.'

As Ron Silver was looking over the 'spec sheets', Jack was talking to Jessica Miles about the introductory offer.

'While Ron is checking out the bearing, Jack, give me your price for a lot of 5000.'

'£4.72 per bearing. When we deduct the introductory 10 per cent, your price becomes £4.25. What do you think?"

'I'll pull the file on the last order; give me a moment please.' Jack was looking forward to this. It was important to keep his eyes on Jessica Miles. He wanted to gauge her facial expression when she looked up the cost on her previous order. This, now, would confirm Jack's strong suspicions about Ben. As Miles flipped through the purchase orders and accompanying invoices, Jack was not disappointed.

'Jack, are you sure your price is correct.?'

'Yes, of course.'

'How much was your previous bearing?'

'£4.72. The reason why we can sell this replacement for the same money is simply due to engineering changes in our production which have cut our costs.'

'Why offer a discount for such a superior product?'

'Well, my company feels that you are a very important prospect. As part of our marketing strategy, we decided to offer a discount to first-time customers so they would be encouraged to try our products. We would like to do business with you.'

'Jessica,' Ron Silver was speaking, 'this bearing looks almost too good to be true. Based on these specifications and test results, I think that we could not only cut our costs dramatically, but we can even enhance our own product guarantee. I'd like to try a batch out with production, and put them to the test.'

'All right Jack. Can you send me a sample order to try out?'

'How many would you like?'

'Say, 100 to begin. We can run our own tests and then decide about the rest of the order.'

'No problem Mrs Miles. If you don't mind, I'll log your order in for 5000 so that we can guarantee you the discount; we can ship you the first 100 by the end of this week. After you've tried these and are happy with the results, we can arrange to ship you the balance.'

'Ron, what do you think?' Miles was looking to her engineer.

'Yes, I think it's a good idea.'

'Done,' Miles confirmed. 'If these work out as well as you claim Jack, we'll be doing a lot of business in the future.'

'Thank you both. You won't regret this.'

Jack was walking through the car park and began to wonder what he would say to Ben when he got back from his holiday. Obviously, he was not going to be pleased with losing out on his 'extra pocket money'. Jack continued mulling over the problem until he said aloud, 'that's it.' He knew that Ben would try to get his old supplier reinstated, however, Jack now had two allies that he would be able to count on – Miles and Silver. Jack would make a point of keeping them updated on special offers and new products simply by writing a letter to Ben with copies to the other two. In fact, he would also have one of his engineers call and speak to Silver, periodically, to get his input. In doing this, Ben would always be hard-pressed to come up with a plausible reason for changing suppliers. 'Jack, my boy, you're in.'

Case 8

The Prevaricator

'Peter Spillman is a real treat,' Jack was thinking as he approached his office in the rear of the warehouse. 'I don't think this dingbat would know what an honest answer was, even if one came up and kicked him where the sun doesn't shine.' Jack himself had thought of doing this on more than one occasion. Peter had the uncanny knack of being able to look someone straight in the eyes and concoct the most absurd statements about his buying habits and abilities. There were times when Jack felt like telling him to see a doctor and get some help; but what use would that be? He'd probably tell him that he had his doctorate and had already written three books on 'psychoanalysis'. No, Peter would have to be dealt with differently. Today, Jack had a plan.

'Pete, good to see you.' Jack was biting his tongue.

'Jack-o, long time no see. Come and rest your weary bones.'

'Thanks Pete. How is everything going?'

'Great. If it got any better, I couldn't stand it. Did I tell you about . . . no I couldn't have. I haven't seen you in months. Jack, you may be dealing with someone else here pretty soon.'

Jack was sure that his heart palpitated at this news. Could it be possible that Pete's company was finally going to hire a real human to do their purchasing? 'Hang-on Jack,' he began to calm himself. 'Pete probably hasn't *really* been invited to join the US space programme; unless, of course, the American government decided to experiment on how long a person would survive in space without a life support system. Ah, go on Jack, bite.'

'You're joking Pete; what's up?'

'You remember I told you that I joined a new golf club last year.'

'Yes, I do.' Jack was getting ready for a good one.

'Well, I've been playing three to four times a week for the last nine months, and the club pro has been keeping an eye on me. In *each* of the last five months, I've had a hole-in-one. One of them, in fact, was a 335 yarder! It was downhill of course.'

'Wow Pete, that's great.'

'Wait a minute, I haven't told you the news yet. The pro said he was going to talk to the owners and see if they are interested in starting up a special clinic: "Swinging for the Hole". If they do, I'm their man.'

'I'm really going to miss you. When will you find out for certain?' Jack eagerly asked the question.

'Probably any day now. In the meantime I suppose I'll just have to slug it out here.'

'Pete, you are a man of amazing talents. Tell me, seeing as you have to wait for the golf thing to "gel", what are you doing in the meantime about your bearing orders for the factory?'

'Same old thing Jack. I'm buying my bearings for a pound and half less than you've offered. I like you a lot though and, you know, I'd give you the business if you could match the price.'

'You're giving me the business all right,' Jack thought, and held back a smile. Although Pete could look him straight in the eyes when he fed Jack this bowl of 'malarkey', he was exhibiting all the other tell-tale signs of dishonesty. First he was tugging at his left ear lobe as he delivered this living testimony to his negotiating skills; who else in modern day business could regularly buy a product at below cost? Next, he crossed his arms and leaned forward. Finally, he began to stroke his chin with his palm, which caused his hand to cover his mouth. 'Pete,' Jack mused to himself, 'you're a classic textbook case. Here is where the fun begins.'

'Pete, I can't believe the ways you come up with these deals. What's your secret?'

'Really no secret. Some companies are a little hungrier for business than others. I only deal with the starving ones!'

'You've got to be just about the best negotiator I have ever come across.'

Pete was smiling. He loved to be praised. Now was the time for Jack to lay down the snares. 'Pete, I'm going to let you step into the jaws of the steel trap, but I'll help you get it off before you hurt yourself irreparably,' Jack was saying to himself. The time had come!

(Phase 1 – Setting the bait)

'Pete, did you mean it before when you said you would give me the business if I could match what you currently pay for your bearings?'

'Jack, old man, would I lie to you?'

'I really appreciate your support, Pete. What I need now is your advice and your help.'

'Ask and you shall receive.'

'First of all, how do you think I should approach my boss on getting him to lower our price? We are talking about a sizeable discount here.'

'Just tell him that he should meet the competition.'

'I know. I've already tried that. What I mean is, how do you think I can convince him that there are people out there, our competitors, who will sell so much lower than we do?'

'Explain to him that . . . how much are your bearings Jack?'

'£4.72.'

'Yes. Explain to him that I get my bearings for around £3.25 a piece, and if he is serious about doing business with us, he has to get serious about his prices.'

'I'll try that. The thing is, £3.25 is below cost, Pete. Let me ask you something. If you owned this company and one of your sales reps came to you and said that you had to go below cost to make a sale, what would you do?'

'Well Jack, wait a minute. First of all, you were the one that said £3.25 was below cost. It may be below your cost, but how do you know it is below everyone else's?'

'We are the largest producer of bearings in the country. We buy raw materials in greater quantities than anyone else. We have patented designs on our machinery, which, industry-wide, is considered to be the most efficient in the field. Our domestic and export markets are large enough to produce significant economies of scale in our production. Finally, we sell more than anyone else which implies that our prices must be fairly good.'

'Jack, I don't deny this, but none the less, there is always someone out there prepared to go lower than the others.'

'Pete, are the bearings you purchase as good as ours? We may not be comparing apples with apples.'

'Ah, no, probably not as good, but good enough.'

'I have to get him to quantify "good enough",' Jack remembered. 'What do you mean "good enough"?' he asked aloud.

'Well, they may not last as long, but they're a lot cheaper.'

'So, you agree that we have the better bearing?'

'Yes.'

'Would you happily change over to us if we could furnish you our bearing at your current price, relatively speaking?'

'If you mean for around the same price, yes, of course.'

(Phase 2 – Springing the trap)

'Peter, that's super. Here's where I need your help. My boss said that we could not afford to be so "out-priced" in the market. He told me before I left on this trip that if I was sure about these pricing anomalies, I should set up a meeting between you, your company president, he and I. It's his intention to meet the competitive price. You're going to be a hero, Pete.

Forget about your golf career; this is going to give you a terrific push up the ladder from right here. I tell you, you've got to be the best purchasing manager I've ever met. Can we all get together next week on Thursday or Friday? My boss, Pat Gormley, told me that he would keep the decks clear for both of those days.'

'Whooaa Jack!'

'What's the problem? Do you want to get together sooner than that?'

'No, it's not that. It's just that I don't know when I can set up a meeting with the old man.'

'Come on Pete. This is no trivial matter. The money that your company will save in a year by purchasing our better bearings will be fantastic.'

Pete looked a little pale. He had himself so deep in the hole that he wouldn't see over the rim even if he were jumping on a trampoline. Jack thought he saw beads of perspiration prior to Pete wiping his brow with his hand. There was a long pause, then finally Pete said, 'Jack, I've got to be honest with you. Mr Slater has already suggested that we should look into buying better bearings. He hasn't been totally satisfied with what we've been using up till now.'

'You mean you may be willing to buy better bearings at the same price as what you are paying, or, are you prepared to pay a little extra?'

'No, in fact I think I can convince "Mr Skinflint" to cough up a little bit more money. He's really hot on making a change.'

(Phase 3 – Releasing the trap)

'If I could offer you another bearing that we produce, which lasts twice as long as anything else in the market, would you be interested?'

'It certainly sounds good.'

'The thing is Pete, we could never sell you that one for £3.25. In theory though, if it lasts twice as long as what you are using, you could pay £6.50 and still enjoy the same competitive position that you do today.'

'No way Jack. I'm not about to pay that much for any bearing.'

'But it has twice the life.'

'Forget it. I agree it would be worth more, but not that much more.'

'I'll tell you what, Pete. Pat Gormley is really keen to get your business. If we could let you have this one for the same price as our old one, would you make the switch?'

'You mean, £4.72?'

'Yes, that's right.'

'I think I could convince Mr Slater that it was a good buy at that price. After all, it does last twice as long.'

'Is that a "yes"?'

'Yes. You'd have a deal.'

'Pete, guess what? I was hoping you would be interested in this better bearing and I talked to Pat about it before I came. He said that if you would switch at this price, I was authorized to offer it to you. When and how many can I deliver?'

'That's pretty slick, Jack. You're good and I like dealing with you. You're my kind of people. Send me a thousand next week.'

'You've got it. Thanks a lot Pete. I'll see you next month. By the way, good luck with your golf game.'

Jack returned to his hotel room. He was afraid that if his grin got any bigger, his lips would fall off. 'I finally beat him at his own game. It's 100 per cent true that "if you give someone enough rope they'll hang themselves".' He continued smiling as he laid his head down to go to sleep. He was heading back tomorrow morning, bright and early. He still had another tough customer to tackle and he sure needed his rest and wits to get by Rupert Rawlings, the Intimidator!

Case 9

The Intimidator

After having enjoyed numerous successes this week, Jack felt he was ready for 'Genghis Khan'. That wasn't this customer's true name, of course, but Jack always fondly referred to him as such. This man could curdle fresh milk just by looking at it. The closest thing that could be construed as his smile, was the expression Mr Rupert Rawlings took when he happened to be having a 'gas attack'. Fortunately, this did not occur often; smiling did not become him. A smile on Rawlings' face was similar to having a rat in your dustbin. It might be there, but no one really wants to look at it. Besides, if you ignored it, it might just go away by itself.

Jack gingerly approached Rawlings' office. He looked both ways in the corridor to ensure that he was still safe. 'There's time to turn back,' was the thought that flashed through Jack's mind. No, he couldn't retreat. It just wasn't possible. Rawlings specifically told him to come by today, and he suffered disobedience very badly. 'All right Jack, the time has come to make your stand – no more cowering.' Jack straightened his back, knocked firmly on the office door and marched straight into the dragon's pit. He was harbouring the hope that, unlike General Custer, this was *not* to be his 'last stand'.

'Good morning Mr Rawlings.'

'Who are you?'

'Jack Average of Totronics sir. You asked me to come by today.'

'What company are you from?'

'Totronics.'

'Ah yes, that's right. Sit.'

Jack extended his hand but Rawlings either didn't see it, or, chose to ignore it. Instead, he got up from his desk, placed his hands on his hips and stared at Jack. 'Is he auditioning for a film on "intimidating body language",' Jack wondered? 'Well, it's not going to work this time.' Jack looked Rupert Rawlings in the eyes, smiled and said, 'What can I do for you today Mr Rawlings?'

'What kind of sales rep are you Average?'

This statement seemed a little like deja-vu to Jack. At times like this he wondered himself just what kind of rep he was. 'Jack, don't succumb to his abuse,' he remembered, 'deal with the facts, not the individual personality.'

Rawlings continued, 'I heard through the grapevine that your company is introducing a new, long-life bearing and I want to know why this information didn't come from you?'

'Mr Rawlings, my secretary sent out the announcements to all of my customers two months ago. I don't believe that you were omitted from the list that I gave her. If, however, your letter was lost in the mail, I do apologize.'

'What's wrong with the telephone?'

'I've tried to get three different appointments with you since then, but your secretary told me that you were too busy to see sales representatives. The last time I phoned, two weeks ago, she told me that you would call me if you needed me.'

Rawlings returned to his seat, propped his elbows up on his desk and joined both his hands at their fingertips. His stare never left Jack's face. Jack, for his part, looked back at 'Genghis', slowly smiled and suggested: 'May I show you the literature on this revolutionary bearing, Mr Rawlings? We feel that this product will cut your costs considerably.'

'Why do you think that I wanted you to come in here? It certainly wasn't to practise synchronized swimming.'

Jack ran through a mental list. 'With this brute, I had better position myself to see all of his miserable body language. I get the feeling that I'll need every edge I can get.' Aloud he said, 'Yes sir. I mean, no sir. I have quite a few interesting brochures and "spec sheets" with me today. Would you mind if I moved my chair to the side of your desk where I could lay these out properly for you to see?'

'Stay where you are.' Rawlings grunted and looked out of his window. 'You know, I've a good mind to call your president and tell him what kind of miserable sales reps he sends me. If you worked for me for five minutes you wouldn't be around to see the sixth.'

'Mr Rawlings, if I can't show you my material and explain it to you, I might as well just post you what I have.'

'That's a good idea . . . get out! I've got no time for salespeople who can't sell.'

'I'm sorry you feel that way. Most of my customers . . .'

'I don't give a damn about most of your customers.'

'Yes I realize that, but none the less, most of my customers appreciate the way that I stay in touch and keep them informed. With your permission however, I'll suggest that my boss assign someone else to take care of your sales needs.'

Jack noticed that, at this comment, Rawlings leaned forward in his chair and opened his hands on his desk. 'Am I actually getting through?' he wondered. 'It's time to appeal to his humanness.'

'Average, no salesperson has ever talked to me like that before. I should physically throw you out of my office.'

'Mr Rawlings, I'm not your enemy. I'm actually a pretty good sales rep because I genuinely try to help my customers. All I wanted to do today was explain to you the benefits of a new market innovation. You know sir, I'm not angry with you for disliking me, I'm upset with myself because somehow I failed to live up to your expectations. For that I'm sorry. I'm not perfect but I'm trying to do my best. Let me leave you these brochures and literature and I'll have my boss, Pat Gormley, give you a call tomorrow.'

Rawlings sat back in his chair and adjusted his glasses. 'Never mind,' he barked, 'you're here now. Go ahead with what you want to talk to me about.'

'Thanks Mr Rawlings, I really appreciate another chance. Before we begin sir, I understand that you are in the process of changing over your entire system of drive shafts on your conveyors so you will gain better energy efficiency with your machines.'

'That's right. Who told you?'

'One of my company engineers. I think that he lives next door to your plant manager.'

'Well I don't imagine it's a big secret. Yes, I'm having them installed next week.'

'I just wanted to say that I think it's a brilliant idea. With rising energy costs, the most progressive companies are beginning to take this route. I think you are demonstrating tremendous foresight.'

'Ah, thanks. Now, let's get down to business.'

Twenty minutes later

'To recap, Mr Rawlings, you said you needed a bearing that can withstand the rigours of machinery which works around the clock, seven days a week.'

'That's right.'

'You want to install bearings that you won't have to change every six months. I think you said that you wanted to avoid all the labour involved, and the down-time that you incur.'

'Yes.'

'Am I also correct in saying that you not only intend to use them in your machinery, but you will also incorporate the bearing in your own manufacturing process for the products that you sell?'

'That pretty well sums it up.'

'Do you feel comfortable with the "specs" that I've shown you? I mean, are you convinced that our tests have given you a fair assessment of what this product can do?'

'I have no reason to doubt your company's word. Totronics has always been a leader in the field.'

'Based on what I've shown you, do you feel that our new bearing will do the job for you?'

'I must admit, I think this would give our production a real shot in the arm.' That was the 'action' buying signal Jack was waiting for.

'Thank you sir. How many can I send you?'

'Hang on a minute. You haven't even told me how much they cost.'

'Mr Rawlings, this bearing will absolutely keep your factory humming. You won't be seeing mechanics in dirty overalls, every six months, taking your machinery to bits. You won't see orders back up during your down-time. You won't be paying operators to stand around. What you will experience is an even better product going out of the door, onto your delivery truck, heading for your waiting customers.'

'I want the bearing. I just don't want to pay the earth for it.'

'How many would you buy if I told you that it's about the same price as what you are already paying to Base for their bearing?'

'Why, I'd buy 5000!'

'Our price, believe it or not, is only £4.72 each. When would you like delivery?'

'That's not bad. Send me the 5000 bearings next Thursday morning.'

'Yes sir. We'll be here bright and early. Thank you.'

'By the way Average, if you want more business from me, you had better keep in touch.'

'Mr Rawlings, believe me, you'll see me as often as you wish to.'

Jack left Rawlings' office in utter disbelief. He was sure he had actually seen a smile on Genghis' face when he told him to 'keep in touch'. 'Yes, he must have smiled,' Jack was convinced. 'He didn't belch the whole time I was in there. Maybe, just maybe, the ogre is human after all!'

Case 10

Rebuilding Burnt Bridges

As the week was winding down, Jack realized that he had one more call to make. It was a visit he would not have conceived of making four days ago but now he believed that he was ready. The time had come to face Jack Jordan. In fact, it was because of the confidence that he gained this week that he felt he could afford to be taken down several notches without being irreparably crushed. 'Several notches, hah,' Jack said to himself, 'he'll probably whittle my head to a fine point.' None the less, Jack knew that Mr Jordan was owed an apology, not just on Jack's behalf but also for the sake of Totronics. The company should not be made to suffer for his blunder. Jack had too many hard-working team members, who deserved a better fate than he had cast for them.

Jack's hands were shaking slightly as he turned off his ignition outside Jordan's office building. Suddenly, something occurred to him: he hadn't heard from Help since the middle of the week. 'Help!' he cried aloud.

'I've been very proud of you this week, Jack.'

'I don't know what I would have done without you. All those clues that you gave me really paid off. Please make sure that you hang around though, and don't wander off like you did a few days ago.'

'Jack, I did no wandering. You were perfectly able to handle the situations that you came across simply by using your skills.'

'Yes, but, you told me what to do and what to say.'

'All that I did for you was open the door to your own knowledge. In effect, the hinges had become rusty through lack of use. Once the door's hinges were oiled, you found yourself quite able to push it open at will.'

'I don't go for all that philosophical stuff. I need you now more than ever.'

'Jack, you're worried about what to say to Mr Jordan. That is perfectly understandable. Repairing a damaged relationship is never easy.'

'No, it's not. I've had to go in to see accounts before who slammed the door on one of our sales reps. I've seen customers who swore that they would never see another Totronic salesman because of what my predecessor had done. Those were relatively easy to overcome. All I had to do was sell myself. Gain their trust. Ask them to give *me* a chance.'

'*Why do you think that this case with Mr Jordan will be much different?*' Help's question opened Jack's eyes.

'I think I see what you mean.'

Jack approached Jordan's receptionist with his head slightly bowed and with a very timid voice asked, 'Would you please ask Mr Jordan if he would see Jack Average for a few minutes? I have something very pressing and personal to talk to him about.' The receptionist disappeared for a brief period and when she returned she informed Jack that Mr Jordan was too busy to see him.

'May I call Mr Jordan from your telephone?'

'Well, I don't think Mr Jordan wishes to be disturbed.'

'Please, Mrs Anderson. I could leave the building and telephone from a call box, but I'd rather do it this way. I'm not trying to get you in trouble, but it is rather important that I speak to Mr Jordan.'

'All right Mr Average. Let me dial his extension.'

'Jack Jordan here, can I help you?'

'Mr Jordan, this is Jack Average. Please hear me out for a moment. I must speak with you personally. I promise that what I have to say will only take a minute or two. I won't bother you again, after that, I swear.'

'Mr Average, I fail to see any reason why you and I should talk, now or at any time in the future.'

'Please, all I need is two minutes of your time and then I'll leave.'

'Very well Mr Average. Two minutes. Ask Mrs Anderson to bring you to my office.'

Jack did so, and Mrs Anderson began leading him down the corridor to the last office on the right. While walking, Jack ran over the scene in his mind of what it was that he was going to say. A simple apology was not enough. Jack tried to trick Jordan and was caught in the act. He needed to ensure that Mr Jordan knew how sorry he was. He needed to convince him of his sincerity. Mrs Anderson knocked and opened the office door. Jack walked in.

'What can I do for you Mr Average? Quite frankly, I'm surprised to see you back here.'

'Well, Mr Jordan, I just wanted to come back and face you personally and tell you how sincerely sorry I am about what happened last Monday. I know I have no right to expect anything except your anger at the way I behaved; however, please believe me when I say that I've never done anything like that before, and I know I'll never do anything like it again.'

'What's the point of your being here now?'

'Mr Jordan, your company is a valued customer to Totronics, and I know that, as a company, we would hate to see you take your business elsewhere. We have many, very good sales representatives, and although I have no right to ask, would it be possible to have someone else call on you? If you agree, I'll talk to my boss and explain to him why we have to remove me from your account.'

'Just out of curiosity, what would you tell your boss?'

'The truth. I've destroyed the trust that we had between us.'

'This leads me to another question. Wouldn't you get yourself in trouble by admitting to that?'

'Yes, probably. The thing is, Totronics is a great company and hopefully they will not have to suffer for my personal blunder.'

'Mr Average, you surprise me again. I didn't get the impression that you were overly concerned with honesty when we met on Monday. Why the sudden change?'

'It's a long story, Mr Jordan. Suffice it to say that I've been having a lot of personal problems lately and I haven't been myself. The one thing I can assure you of is the fact that I am an honest person. What I did earlier was totally out of character.'

'Why did you try to trick me? Why did you try to sell me basically outdated stock?'

'Mr Jordan, throughout my working career in sales I have kept the customer's needs in mind. These needs have always come first for me. I have just come through a period where I was more confused than I ever have been in my life. When I saw you on Monday, basically I had already "bottomed out"; I've never been so low. I sat up Monday night trying to figure out what direction I should take with my life, and then I spent this entire week trying to get it together again. I may not be all the way back yet, but I'm well on my way. I intend to be as good for my customers as I always aspired to be. One of the things that I discovered when I was doing my soul searching was that, for me to be first, I have to place my customers and my company's interests ahead of my own. I don't intend to fail.'

Jack Jordan sat back in his chair and stroked his chin. He didn't speak for a moment, but looked deeply in to the eyes of this individual sitting in front of him. What he saw was genuine honesty and sincerity. What he saw was a real human being capable of making mistakes. He also saw a true apology.

'Jack, we all make mistakes. It takes someone with real character to do what you have just done. I believe you when you say that you did what you did in exceptional circumstances. I know. I've been pretty low myself at one point in my life and I too did things that I wouldn't have ordinarily done. I don't think that I need another sales rep from Totronics calling on me. I think I can trust the one who is here. Let's start afresh,

Jack. Come by and see me again next week and we'll take a look at some of your new products!'

'Mr Jordan . . .'

'Call me Jack,' and Jordan smiled.

'Jack, I can't thank you enough for this second chance. You'll never regret it. See you next week.'

This week completed the cycle for Jack Average. He had overcome his fears, anxiety and lack of self-confidence. As he said to Jack Jordan, he may not be all the way back, but he is heading in the right direction. With a little bit of help he will succeed.

Epilogue
Jack on the Road to Rediscovery

Jack got home Friday nght feeling a sense of relief that he hadn't felt for months, maybe years. He wasn't sure if it was relief, elation or plain 'old fashioned' satisfaction at having done a good job over the last four days. This week had been a week of rediscovery for him. Jack was now certain that his cloudy vision about himself and his career was acutely focused.

On Monday morning Jack was first to arrive at his office . . . except for Pat Gormley. Pat was sitting beside Jack's desk reading the sports section of the newspaper. The moment he saw Jack enter, he stood and without expression asked, 'Jack, can I see you in my office?'

'Well Jack my boy, it seems you played a little too hard last week with some of the accounts,' he thought to himself. 'Was it Jordan who called the office last Tuesday to complain? No, I don't think so. He would have said something to me on Friday. Maybe it was old man Mitchell. He said he had a mind to call the president, Mr Miller. If he had a mind at all he would have done something there and then. No, besides, he told me to stay in touch when I left him. It must have been big, bad Rupert Rawlings. I must have been a little too rough there. I'm not sure he appreciated my direct approach; probably too human for him. Well, what the hell. I said what I believed, and it needed to be said, if not by me then by someone else. That horse's ass has no right to treat people the way he does. I am a little surprised though. I really believed that I got through to him. According to everything I've read, studied and remember about selling a bully, I did the only thing that I could do. Forget it, maybe I'll see him in another life. If I do, I'll put a laxative in his tea. He might as well have verbal diarrhoea to go along with his verbal abuse.'

'Of course Pat, what's up?'

'What did you do last week when you were up north?'

'I saw a lot of accounts, why?'

'I can't believe you, that's why. I really thought that I knew your character pretty well; probably better than most in fact. But, I'll tell you Jack, you even surprised me.'

Jack's mind was racing at 100 mph. 'What do you think Jack? Should you quit now or wait for him to lower the boom? I like Pat and I don't want to make it harder for him than it has to be. All right, time to do the honourable thing.'

'Pat listen, about last week, I really tried to get my act together and . . .'

'Get your act together! What you did was comparable to a centre forward going 20 matches without scoring a goal and then erupting with 10 goals in five games. I've never seen anything like it. First Fred Herbert called and booked a sizeable order. Jack, he's been one of your target accounts for close to three years. Then, Mr Mitchell telephoned me personally to place an order. He said if we ever removed you from his account, neither he nor his ancestors would ever do business with us again. Next, Rupert Rawlings fired in an order for 5000 bearings. Jack, I hate to admit it, but in all the time that I had him for one of my accounts he never gave me anything but grief. Frankly, I never expected to see an order from him in this lifetime. Finally Jack, the people over at Malbay called Miller and told him that we could do their entire plant renovation if you were personally involved. They said that they like doing business with a company as committed to quality as they are. I don't know how or what you did, but congratulations. Whatever happened to you last week should happen to the entire salesforce.'

Jack sat back in his chair with his mouth agape, unable to speak. Here he was expecting to be stoned to death; instead he was being buried under the weight of the flowers being thrown upon him.

'*Jack, remember to accept praise the same way you should accept criticism . . . with grace. A good week, or a bad one does not make or break a career. Keep a perspective about the fundamentals and how important they are to your chosen profession. Even the best salespeople have their ups and downs. Learn to take your "ups" down and bring your "downs" up. You are as good as you believe you are and no one sale call is going to change that.*'

Pat was talking now. 'Jack, you seem to have not only recaptured your old form, but actually surpassed it. I just wanted to catch you early this morning, before our sales meeting, to ask you what your secret is?'

'It's not a secret, Pat. I just recently remembered how to succeed at the oldest profession in the world.'

Jack sat down this week and wrote thank you postcards to everyone he saw the week before. He especially thanked Mr Mitchell and explained that these postcards would become one of the ways that he would stay in touch. Finally, Jack decided to do something special for Lou Grover.

Lou Grover sat in his office the following Monday morning and opened a curious looking package that was lying on his desk. He opened it carefully, half expecting an exploding gift from his brother

Rob (it ran in his family). To his relief, it seemed to be a T-shirt with a card attached from Jack Average. He unfolded it, held it up and let out a riotous laugh that shook every gizmo in the place. The T-shirt was inscribed:

IVQII
LOU

Conclusion

I sincerely hope that you have enjoyed this section of the book. These case studies were deliberately kept short so that the approach could be examined without getting unnecessarily complicated with a lot of dialogue. I'm sure you'll agree there could have been other ways to solve the same problem and achieve the same results. This is why reviewing the basics, which we do in Part 2, is so important. They will stimulate and promote other ideas which help to keep you sharp. They represent rungs on the sale ladder. The more adept you are at negotiating the rungs, the higher you will climb.

You may be wondering who or what the voice was that assisted Jack in his comeback. That, too, is fairly simple. It is not an imaginary, science fiction or fantasy-type character. It is also not poetic license in creating something to help the story along. That voice is real! The voice comes from knowing the basic skills of the trade so intimately that they are instinctive. The voice is something we all have. The voice is *your conscience*!

Part 2

Back to basics

1

Selling and What it Takes

PERSONAL ATTRIBUTES

To conform or not to conform; that is the question. The answer, however, is mixed. Since we live in society, it is obvious that we must all conform to a basic set of rules of behaviour. Let's be thankful for that. What occurs in many cases in business, however, is that this conformity is taken well beyond its useful limits to a point where it stifles creativity. It is a fine line we have to walk between what is expected of us and what is progressive.

Paradoxically, no company of which I am aware wants their ranks filled with automatons. A growth company needs new and fresh ideas. So what happened? Well, in my opinion, it's what most people have come to accept as being true: don't rock the boat, don't buck the system. Unfortunately, because of this many people tend to go out of their way to become inconspicuous. We as salespeople, however, cannot fall into any such homogeneous group. We need to be individuals – people who stand out.

Every individual is unique, and it is this uniqueness that we should explore and cultivate. Being unique is one of our most important tools in being a complete salesperson. Eagles don't flock!

The key to successful selling then is that each of us accepts ourselves for what and who we are. Trying to be another person's clone doesn't work. If we are truly able to assess our strengths and weaknesses, we can also accept those things that are beyond our abilities. This introspection isn't easy to develop, but if we succeed here, the self-confidence and self-assurance we gain will help overcome more obstacles than we would have believed possible. The ability to accept mistakes and failure, without being overcome by them, places us in total control. It is not enough to say that a proper mental attitude is important in sales – it is paramount!

The first 50 per cent in selling is human relations. We shouldn't delude ourselves with the idea that good skills in dealing with people are either natural, or they are not. This is simply not the case. We must both learn and practise this talent. It may be tough, but we have to cast aside the 'me first' attitude and place more emphasis on the importance of what someone else may think and their perceptions. It may not always be easy to do this, but when it comes to dealing with customers it is always necessary.

To be a good salesperson requires that you be a good amateur psychologist. It means that you must get involved and close to your customers and make them feel good about themselves. Think for a moment about friends of yours who make you feel good about yourself. Don't you like being with them and wouldn't you do things for them that you wouldn't ordinarily do for others? Well, customers are no different when it comes to dealing with a salesperson who puts them in this positive frame of mind. By putting your customer first, you both become winners.

In selling we have to like people even if they don't like us. I guess the mere thought of liking someone who doesn't like your face or the sound of your voice may seem a little strange. The point is, if you genuinely like someone, they will frequently come to like you. This may sound absurd but it's not. After all, have you ever continued to dislike somebody who showed you kindness, consideration and understanding? I doubt it. This is not human nature. When it comes to selling we must adopt the 'you' approach and attitude. It is the only one that works.

Dale Carnegie philosophized that we could make more friends in a fraction of the time simply by being more interested in others instead of trying to get them interested in us. There is a lot of wisdom in this. It isn't difficult to become a likeable person. Being natural, remembering the little details, complimenting honestly and being more ready to build people up instead of knocking them down – all of these factors contribute to our being the kind of person that others feel comfortable with. It involves sincerity. Everyone, and this includes our customers, can quickly spot the difference between true behaviour or pretentious acting on our part. Believe me, to be a success in selling we must have the ability to convince people. To convince people, we must be sincere.

As important as it is to be sincere, there is a second fundamental characteristic needed when dealing with our prospects – *enthusiasm*. It is an ally whose force is of such magnitude that any salesperson who possesses it, can outperform even better equipped salespeople who do not. Probably more than any other virtue, enthusiasm can make the difference between an average and an excellent achiever. It's also contagious. It denotes success and people like to be associated with successful people.

The third quality found in all professionals in our field is *empathy*. It is that ability to mentally place yourself in someone else's position; to truly understand where they are coming from. If a salesperson cannot do this, he or she is not selling up to their true potential. We all have within us the capacity for empathy. Qualities such as kindness, compassion, optimism, thoughtfulness and understanding are examples. The reason some people can communicate empathy where others cannot is quite simple. The people who can are not afraid of revealing genuine emotion when the situation warrants it. Unfortunately, in business, many people guard their privacy to the point of almost stifling any display of sensitivity to others. Good salespeople know, however, that to get close to their customers they must first allow their customer to get close to them. There may always be a risk attached to opening up to people, but the benefits far outweigh the perils.

Finally the fourth fundamental characteristic we need is *dedication*. With it, goals can be accomplished. Without it, they cannot. Vince Lombardi was probably one of the greatest coaches involved in any team sport when he built an American football dynasty in Green Bay, Wisconsin during the 1960s. He judged that dedication required a complete belief in what a person does. If something is worth accomplishing, it should be done to the utmost of one's ability. He was quoted as saying: 'The quality of a person's life is in direct proportion to their commitment to excellence regardless of their chosen field of endeavour.' In sales, this commitment, this dedication, is what we need to realize even our loftiest ambitions.

When we recap our four essential traits to effective selling, we produce the acronym S E E D:

> **S** incerity
> **E** nthusiasm
> **E** mpathy
> **D** edication

All we need do, is plant that seed in the field of perseverance and nourish it daily to sow our future selling success.

Salespeople, as you can imagine, come in all shapes and sizes and from very diverse backgrounds. There are, however, many similarities found among the best: good working habits, understanding of people, motivation, initiative and a creative imagination are several examples. Moreover, the successful individuals are honest and have a keen desire to help solve their customer's problems. Although it would be logical to think that your customer would help you when you are trying to help him, don't always count on it. There is no guarantee that he will supply any facts, true or otherwise. Frequently, your prospect will either believe that certain facts are not important, or he just doesn't want to divulge them. It is like expecting your doctor to know what the trouble is without your offering any clues. You will sometimes need a great deal of patience and perseverance before you get through. It is up to the professional to get down to the core issues, and to communicate them to the customer! Be a problem solver.

Of course, good salespeople must be good communicators. This is especially true when you are trying to work out what needs to be sold, or better yet, what your prospect is going to buy. To communicate with everybody means that you will have to adapt your presentation to the level of the individual you are selling to. Use the power of words to ensure that your message is clear and understood by your prospect.

Although we will be reviewing control factors in a later chapter, it is worthwhile to mention here several characteristics that salespeople should master:

- *Tension*. It is imperative that we always appear to be at ease. If we are not, it's a safe bet that our customer won't be either. If the prospect isn't relaxed, he or she is unlikely to buy anything – including what it is that we are trying to sell.
- *Disturbing mannerisms*. If we have any nervous habits, or what others may consider to be insufferable mannerisms, it is best to get these under control. Rarely will a prospect see someone who irritates him.
- *Courtesy*. The need for courtesy is obvious, but it should never be taken to the point of being effusive.
- *Emotions*. Notwithstanding my earlier comments on showing emotion when exhibiting empathy (which is an entirely different situation), it is always best to maintain our composure when dealing with a client. This rule particularly applies when we receive either very good or very bad news from her. We cannot overreact to anything we hear. Rather, we have to maintain our poise. It is far better for our activities to control our thoughts, rather than the reverse.

Frequently, to keep our emotions in check requires not only self control, but also diplomacy. Diplomacy, as defined for salespeople, is the art of thinking twice before saying nothing. Loosely translated, it means that we won't be criticized for something we didn't say!

Diplomacy alone is not enough though. It is like trying to clap with one hand. We also need tact. Tact is the art of making a point without making an enemy. Winning an argument and losing a customer is not a very rewarding experience.

Cultivating diplomacy and tact is not at all complicated. It only requires that a person be slow to criticize, asking for rather than demanding something, and using the three most powerful words in the English language: 'please' and 'thank you'.

Some final points on the personal attributes found in the better salespeople are that they:

- are on time for appointments;
- enjoy meeting and talking to people;
- believe that a job worth doing is worth doing well;
- are absolutely reliable;
- don't leave things to the last minute;
- are quick starters;
- are relaxed and self-confident in the company of others;
- keep their promises regardless of personal inconvenience;
- honour their commitments;
- believe in business before pleasure;
- enjoy entertaining people;
- enjoy challenges; and
- use their alarm clocks.

Moreover, the professional has the ability to keep things in perspective. Salespeople meet with a great deal of rejection when dealing with customers, but the reality of rejection is counterbalanced by their anticipated, and inevitable, successes. You see, success and rejection are both integral parts of the selling game.

ATTITUDE TRAITS

In sales, probably more than any other profession, a positive attitude is the foundation for a flourishing career. With it, our limits are few and our opportunities are many. Norman Vincent Peale, the author of the best seller, *The Power of Positive Thinking*, had this to say: 'A man who is self-reliant, positive, optimistic and undertakes his work with the assurance of success magnetizes his condition. He draws to himself the creative powers of the universe.' This type of attitude is not only dynamic, as Mr Peale pointed out, it is also contagious.

Those who expect to win, generally do. When we speak positively and optimistically around others, we often find them echoing and reinforcing our outlook. Conversely, how often do we hear people complain about their insurmountable problems and bad luck, only to see them extract these same sentiments from others? These people are frequently chronic pessimists and we are best to keep our distance to avoid being dragged down into their abyss. Anyone who thinks defeat and expects the worst usually gets both.

We in sales have the advantage with a positive attitude. Where a defeatist sees only problems, we see opportunities. We believe that for every problem there is a solution if we take the time to find it. Also, we realize that there are going to be a lot of 'mini failures' on our road to success because this must be expected. What we don't do, is turn a small setback into a true disaster by overstating its importance. We learn to accept disappointment without being overcome by it.

In fact, it isn't really difficult to overcome most problems. The secret lies in our insistence on success and our refusal to concede defeat. We should start by extracting negative words from our vocabulary. Words like: quit, cannot, unable, impossible, out of the question, improbable, unworkable, hopeless, retreat and failure are all examples of negativism. We certainly don't need them in our profession.

The most important fact to remember is that nobody can be a failure unless he or she consent to it. I came across a poem written by Edgar Guest, which best embraces this concept:

> *No one is beat 'til he quits*
> *No one is through 'til he stops*
> *No matter how failure hits*
> *No matter how often he drops.*
> *A fellow's not down 'til he lies*
> *In the dust and refuses to rise.*
> *Fate can slam him and bang him around*
> *And batter his frame 'til he's sore*
> *But it never can say that he's downed*
> *While he bobs up serenely for more.*
> *A fellow's not dead 'til he dies,*
> *Nor beat 'til he no longer tries.*

SETTING GOALS

Despite a fiercely competitive business climate, top sales people continually lead in their respective fields. It is no coincidence that this should be so, it's simply a question of focusing their attention on an objective – a goal. Without a goal we haven't a plan, and without a plan we haven't a chance. Anyone who wishes to place their fate in the hands of lady luck should be prepared to accept the consequences.

I have heard many people talk about their bad luck and how others always seem to have so much good luck; this is ludicrous! People generally make their own luck. If it seems that the same individuals have an uncanny knack of always enjoying good fortune, it is only because they have the will to overcome misfortune. We could say this another way: when opportunity meets preparation, positive things result. Having goals and being alert to opportunities spells success.

Everybody, not just salespeople, should set goals for the day, the week, the month, the year and well beyond. A goal provides us with a course – it keeps us focused. It also helps us to identify the problem area if we become untracked. In setting goals, it is best to remember that we have to stick our necks out if we are to be seen over the crowd. This means that our ambitions should be high enough that we must stretch our capabilities in order to achieve them.

Goals should be practical, as well as attainable. If we set our goals too high we may end up conceding the issue before the challenge begins. Conversely, if we set them too low we can never hope to develop and grow as individuals. It is more important to surpass our own achievements rather than to try to surpass those of others. No matter what may be said about the importance of setting goals, there is one fact of life upon which we can depend: there is absolutely no value in setting a goal if it is not followed through with *decisive action*.

LEARNING TO RELAX

In the last few years there has been a great deal written about the effects of stress and worry. People have come to accept the value of relaxation and are now doing things that they have never done before. More and more individuals are getting involved in hobbies and are taking the time to enjoy their leisure periods with their families and friends. I believe that everyone today realizes that a person isn't really successful if they make a great deal of money and have neither the time nor the health to enjoy it.

The first rule for relaxation is that you leave your work problems at work and your domestic problems at home. If you try to mix the two, you will probably finish by contaminating both aspects of your life.

Rule number two is to spend a quiet time every day and let your mind go blank; I mean completely void, like a vacuum. Do this anywhere that you can find peace and quiet: the park, at home, even your office (just close the door). Take five or ten minutes and concentrate on nothing.

Third, don't get angry and stay angry. Blow off whatever steam you have to, then forget it. Even worse than this is bearing a grudge. The time, frustration and energy wasted here can be put to more productive and positive use elsewhere.

The fourth, and the most important cornerstone in learning to relax, is to develop the ability to accept our limitations. Use what you have been endowed with and do your absolute best with those talents. To do less is tantamount to self-betrayal; to attempt to do more can lead to great frustration and under-achieving. If you consider it for a moment this is not a contradiction of what I had to say earlier.

Strive to avoid stress and worry. According to *The Oxford English Dictionary*, 'worry' is derived from an Anglo-Saxon word meaning 'to choke', or to 'strangle'. Isn't this exactly what worry can do to our minds? If we think about it objectively, is there any logical reason why we should waste any of our valuable time worrying about anything? Either it happens or it doesn't! If what we were worried about unfortunately happens, it is obvious that our worry didn't prevent it from occurring. On the other hand, if nothing happened at all, we shouldn't have worried about it in the first place. If you find yourself troubled about something, think about these concepts:

- Will it matter 50 years from now?
- No matter what happens, we'll all get over it eventually.
- We are at our funniest when we take ourselves too seriously.

I suppose the moral here is that we should always do our best and live for today. Yesterday is history and tomorrow is like a promissory note – we can't change one, and we have no guarantees from the other. So, relax.

2
Positive Praxis

APPOINTMENTS

An item which is generally common to any successful sales story is an alarm clock. Get into the habit of having an early start. The sooner you are out making contact with the customers, the sooner you will have your first opportunity to sell. Try to get that first morning meeting scheduled as early as possible.

More than a few salespeople that I have known have questioned the merits of selling by appointment versus showing up on someone's doorstep and asking to see him or her. Personally, I have always felt that only orphans and puppies show up on doorsteps. Professionals make sure in advance that they are going to be let in. There may be some (very few) disadvantages to making appointments in advance, but there are a host of good reasons why you should. For example:

1. your customer will be there;
2. he will allocate time to see you;
3. making an appointment makes him feel important;
4. it gives him time to prepare;
5. it allows you to gather information over the phone;
6. it gives you time to properly prepare;
7. it allows you to regulate your schedule;
8. it puts you in control;
9. it shows respect for your customer's time; and
10. it gives you a professional image.

When you are setting up your appointments, try to get as general a time as possible: early, mid- or late-morning or afternoon. In this way you won't feel the need to rush through appointments, or leave before you are truly ready. Also your chances of being late for an appointment scheduled for a general time of day are greatly reduced. For example, mid-morning can be anywhere between 9.30 am and 11 am. If however your customer wants to specify a time, accept it and schedule a little extra time in your call immediately preceding his. When you find yourself running late for a meeting, make the effort to call ahead and tell your account. The gesture is appreciated.

Another important point about making appointments is to always behave in a confident manner and expect to be seen. Don't give the impression that time spent with you is time wasted. After all, you are making a special trip to see your prospect and offer your expertise. If you get the feeling that you are either telephoning or seeing your customer at a bad time, don't continue. Make another appointment and call later when the situation has improved. By doing this your message will at least be heard and registered.

A cardinal rule of appointment-making is that once you have a meeting time set up, *never*, positively *never*, call your customer back to reconfirm. If you do, you run the risk of his cancellation. Believe me, this happens more often than you may think. Besides, you have better things to do with your time than to go over work you have already done.

PERSEVERANCE

Getting through to people who are often unavailable can be pretty exasperating. One of the best ways that I have found to do this is to cultivate a rapport with your prospect's assistant. He or she, if feeling so inclined, can guide you in the right direction and help to open up seemingly impregnable doors.

You might also try another approach. The next time that you are in a long-distance area, place a person-to-person call to your client (these calls are almost always put through). If he or she suspects a ruse on your part, simply say that you are out on the road and are trying to set up your schedule for next week. If this seems pretty weak, don't worry about it; at least you have made contact. Now get the appointment!

This brings to mind an experience I had years ago with a new sales recruit. Jerry came to see me and very dejectedly told me that one of his accounts could not, or would not, see him. He refused normal appointments, lunches, dinners, football games . . . everything. It was then that I suggested that Jerry get a breakfast meeting set up. After all, if someone doesn't eat lunch or supper they surely must have breakfast, or at least a cup of coffee.

The very next day, Jerry came in to see me sporting a smile that looked as if someone had jammed a rugby football in his mouth sideways. He proudly announced that he and I had a confirmed breakfast appointment with Mr hard-to-get for the following Monday. I told him that was good work, got out my appointment book and asked Jerry for the time and place; 4.30 am!?! Around the corner from his office. All right, no problem.

The following Monday morning, having had only enough sleep to realize that it had hardly been worth my while going to bed on Sunday night, Jerry and I finally got to see this guy. As incredible as it may seem, not only did we have breakfast together, he actually gave us a two-hour plant tour, spent a total of four hours with us and within two months we had all of his business, lock, stock and barrel.

The customer's reasoning for giving us all of his business (when he never even wanted to see us in the first place), was quite simple. He felt that our perseverance was unique and he figured that salespeople keen enough to do what we did would also be keen enough to make sure that everything went letter perfect with his orders. The lesson here is that perseverance will pay off; you can bank on it.

CUSTOMERS COME FIRST

In any dealings that you have with your customers, it is best to remember that they are not your opponents; they are your bread and butter. By sticking to the fundamental rules of selling, you can assure yourself of continued expansion within your territory. Analyse your customer's needs and *sell benefits* with enthusiasm and sincerity. Listen to your account. She may be trying to tell you how to make the sale. Conduct your presentation so that you arouse interest. Provide adequate explanations. Talk from her point of view. *Give your prospect a reason to buy*.

Once you have done these things, recap your presentation concentrating on the benefits and ask for the business. If your customer turns you down, find out what point(s) she hasn't been sold on yet and start again. When you sense the time is right, ask for the business once more. The key point here is that you don't stop trying.

Repeat the last two steps until you obtain a 'yes'. If, however, you reach a point where you have exhausted all of your available approaches and the account still won't buy, keep the door open to you. Sooner or later your professionalism will win out.

Any time that you promise a customer something, be it a letter, sample delivery, checking on an order, or anything, you had better make good on your commitment. Nothing detracts from your reliability faster than not following through. When a buyer asks you for information, ensure that it is responded to quickly. If you can't reply within the promised time-frame, for whatever reason, phone your account and say so. Even if you don't have his answer yet, you do illustrate to him that you are conscientious and honest. He will appreciate both.

The next item is really a pet peeve of mine – keeping a customer waiting on the line. Often someone may answer your phone and say, 'just a minute please', and then mysteriously forget to mention that someone is holding for you. These individuals seem oblivious to the fact that salespeople must talk to their customers in order to get business.

Try to delegate answering the telephone to someone that you can trust, and who will:

1.   tell your customer you are unavailable at the moment;
2.   tell the client when *you* can call back; and
3.   (taadah!!!) deliver the message to you.

Once you *do* get the message, return the call immediately. Don't have your secretary get your customer on the line and then pass the call through. You're not the boss, your customer is! If he or she is not there when you return the call, leave your name and find out when you can try again. The three rules for handling customers are:

1.   follow-up;
2.   follow-up;
3.   follow-up.

If it is practical, have someone in your office do all of your inside sales work with and for your customers. This individual will probably get to know your accounts' quirks almost as well as you do; the advantages are innumerable. You should set up routine checks with your office when out visiting customers. Try to call in at least twice a day, mid-morning and mid-afternoon. If time permits, also check your messages at lunchtime and at the end of the day. In this way, you can be assured that you are keeping current with the day's events in the office and with your customers.

Any time your customer asks a question about another product or service, or raises an objection to something you have said, it is imperative that you handle this immediately, as well as honestly. If you don't have the product that your customer really needs, don't hesitate to explain where it may be found, even if it means suggesting your competition (remember Case 4). You are a problem solver. You are in it for the long term. Even though you lose this one order, this kind of unselfish act will win you a loyal and long-term customer. I am not suggesting that you should go out of your way to promote your competition or their products; I am talking about those rare cases where *nothing else* is going to do the job. You have only two choices: you can either let your customer flounder, or you can be a problem solver. When you solve a customer's problem with such a demonstration of honesty, you can bet that your statements will be believed again in the future. As Ralph Emerson once said, 'Nothing astonishes men as much as common sense and plain dealing.'

YOUR TIME – YOUR INVESTMENT

You should review your records regularly to see who is buying and who is not. You may find it an interesting concept to sort out your customers by age, sex, colour, type of company and nationality (if applicable), to see if a pattern of buyers versus non-buyers develops. You may be astonished by the results. Also, make sure that records reflect current information. Have you told all interested buyers about new sales promotions, company innovations, product improvements, etc? It *pays* to keep your customers well informed.

Occasionally after a call, you may find yourself with some spare time. This is an ideal opportunity to call in at the company across the street who you suspect may be a prospective buyer. These 'cold-calls' as they are known, can sometimes give you a pleasant surprise. Cold-calls, or a better description 'unscheduled calls', (you are never cold), should not be shied away from under these circumstances.

Although we have already reviewed the importance of making appointments and not just popping in on people, this case is different. You are showing initiative by checking out a new company. As this is a first visit, you are only asking the individual in charge if it is worthwhile to schedule an appointment and, if so, is now suitable? What is more important, you are in the right place at the right time.

A question that is frequently asked by many salespeople is, 'How many calls do I make on a prospect before giving up?' Quite frankly, there is no clear-cut answer here. Much depends on how the prospect is warming up to you, your company and your products. Only you can be the judge of that.

The closest we can come to answering the question, is by asking another question. What is the return on investment? In other words, is the sales volume or potential sales volume worth the time that you must invest to secure it? I have always found that I can best figure this out by seeing myself as an independent businessman who can only make a living by investing his time where he will see results. Results = money. If you have been giving away your time to a non-productive account who offers no good prospects for the future, looking at your time in this way will help to clarify the issue. You will fast become your own favourite charity.

THE WINNING SPIRIT

It is important not to let yourself become intimidated by a customer. It doesn't matter if he or she is a high-ranking company official or someone who looks as if they could use telephone poles for toothpicks. On either extreme, the reason they agree to see you in the first place is that they believe that you may have something interesting to offer them. So, in effect, you are the one in control. Develop a good, strong presentation and practise it. Follow the Vince Lombardi credo, 'Practice does not make perfect; perfect practice makes perfect.'

Lombardi had five basic rules for winning football games that can help us in winning sales:

1. Fatigue makes cowards of us all.
2. Mental toughness is essential to success.
3. Control the ball.
4. Operate on Lombardi time (this means be early and don't waste time).
5. Make a second effort (and a third and a fourth . . .).

Another principle that Lombardi believed in was that of teamwork. You are on a team whether you realize it or not. It is up to you to work with others, learn from others, help others and be helped by others. It is unnecessary to rely on your talents alone when you can draw from supporting co-workers. Observe the successful salespeople around you and ask them questions. Find out what it is that they are doing right.

Just prior to seeing your prospect, make it a rule to look in a mirror. Is this the look you want your customer to see? Is the expression on your face the one which you want to be read? If yes, good! If no, now is the time to change either or both. Look professional, act professional and psyche yourself up for this call. Once you are sitting down in your prospect's office, *never* begin by apologizing for being there. A buyer who doesn't buy isn't wasting his or her time but a seller who doesn't sell is. Also never ask if your client is having a problem with your company. If your customer has a problem, he or she will tell you voluntarily. If you ask, however, your prospect may just try to think of one where none existed before.

When you get into your car in the morning, does it look as if you are running an advertisement for the local car wash? If so, is it the before or the after look? You may not think it is important but many people believe that 'small things' like this provide them with an inside look at the real you. Keep your car's image, and yours, clean.

Finally, before we end this chapter, I should mention something about what to do when you're not in the mood to leap over tall buildings in a single bound. We all feel down on occasion and it is vitally important that we remedy this as quickly as possible.

I have always found that the quickest 'pick-me-up' is to buy myself a nice present. I'm not talking about beach front property in the Caribbean or a Rolex. I mean something small like a pen or a folder or a wallet. Even though it may seem as if this is the time when you can least afford to buy yourself a gift, in fact, the opposite is true. This is the time when you can least afford not to! How you feel is how you sell. Feel good and sell well.

3

Selling – What's Involved?

DEFINING MARKETING AND SALES

Marketing is truly a multifaceted field of study. It is one that is frequently confused with the art of selling. Although marketing and sales do go hand in hand, it is best to understand that selling is only one component of the bigger picture.

Marketing covers every function in the process of getting a product or service from the manufacturer to the consumer. Within this broad scope we deal with:

1. market research;
2. product design;
3. planning market strategy;
4. pricing;
5. advertising and promotion;
6. selection of distribution outlets;
7. physical distribution; and
8. selling.

Although our job is to sell what has been produced, we should be aware of how the total system works. Why? Because, if there is a major defect in one or more of the links in the marketing chain, our chances of successfully selling our product will either be greatly reduced, or eliminated altogether. It is also not fair, nor wise, to think that it is the planner's job to give us what we need to sell effectively. Believe it or not, it is our job to tell the planners what they should be planning for. The onus lies with the salesforce to communicate the wants and needs of the marketplace. There is no one else in the organization close enough to the action to know what these are.

As salespeople, let's concentrate on several key areas where we must give our input to the marketing department. These include the analysis of:

1. market size;
2. customer analysis;
3. selecting a target market;
4. outlining a market strategy;

5.   sales analysis;
6.   sales forecasting; and
7.   competitive analysis.

MARKET SIZE

The worst assumption that you can make when you take over someone's territory is that you are getting a well defined piece of real estate. Chances are you are not. So the first job should be to analyse the territory, determine who the accounts are and what their potential is. This must include business prospects as well as existing base accounts. As you go through this exercise, do not become too alarmed at the lack of information that you find in the files. This phenomenon is the rule, rather than the exception. Instead of being deterred, get determined.

Begin by allocating a specific day, or certain hours every week, when you can devote the time to bringing your account profiles up to date. Many customers or prospects can be qualified quickly by making phone calls. (Do not confuse this with actual face-to-face selling. All that you are trying to do here, is to get a quick handle on your new stomping ground.) Continue this process of definition, include all information that you acquire from your sales calls, and before long you will feel more comfortable about going out to see accounts. Until you define your territory and know who your customers are, it is not unnatural to feel as if you are trying to take off with a 747 on a short runway, in the fog. In effect, this is what you are doing. Without this information you are taking a journey into the unknown.

CUSTOMER ANALYSIS

This is a simple yet complex study. It is simple insofar as it involves getting basic information about your customer. Details such as products purchased, potential sales volumes and decision makers, are usually discovered quickly. It becomes slightly more complex when we expand the job to include determining which products they manufacture, who they compete against and how they sell.

Although this may appear to be a little more information than you actually need, I can assure you that having this knowledge will pay dividends down the road. Also, it is best to realize early on that you will never completely finish this job. Your profile is a living document. Times change, companies change, people change. What you want to accomplish here is the establishment of a system for an ongoing update of your accounts. You should get into the habit of revising the profile after every sales call and include in your updates anything that you have read about the company and/or their industry.

SELECTING A TARGET MARKET

A target market, by definition, is one where we segregate from the whole a fairly homogeneous group of customers, and then develop a strategy to expand our sales penetration within this group. If this sounds like pretty sophisticated stuff, it is. However, it becomes more than worthwhile when you see your sales figures grow and your salary along with them.

In the past, companies used what is commonly known as the 'shotgun' approach. They tried to blanket an entire market by advertising every conceivable selling point that they had to offer. The belief was that the individual customer would pick out the selling point(s) that he could be sold on and then . . . he'd sell himself!? As the saying goes, 'sometimes it works, sometimes it don't.'

Today, however, most companies have elected to take the more precise, 'rifle' approach. They pick out a fairly homogeneous group whose interests are common to each other, and then target their message to these people, using the selling points that they will be sold on. Not only are the results better, but they are also more measurable and less costly to obtain.

There are a few points that should be considered when you want to identify a target market:

- **Market size** It's your territory.
- **Needs** All customer's needs must be identified according to products or services.
- **Segmentation** Divide your market by groups of customer needs.
- **Other data** Add additional information based on existing needs.

OUTLINING A MARKET STRATEGY

Step number one is fairly obvious: pick a target market. Next, create an appropriate mix. A marketing mix isn't very difficult. We combine a list of controllable variables in an effort to satisfy our target group (stay with me now). We've got four basic controllable variables. They are: product, place, promotion and price – the four ps of marketing.

Product

What do you sell?
What advantages do you have over your competition?
Is it innovative?
Will your product give your customer an edge in marketing his own product?

Place

You obviously can't be in more than one place or area at a time. You should keep this in mind when you pick a target group. If you have a cluster of accounts from this group in one area, and others scattered throughout your territory, you may be forced to drop the far away outsiders. After all, the point in developing a target market is to place extra sales emphasis on a specific group so that you end up with more business. You can't do this effectively when you are all over the map. Besides, your target accounts are only one of your responsibilities. You still have a vast territory with regular customers that you can't afford to ignore.

Promotion

Will the product be advertised?
Will special literature be needed?
Will a telephone blitz be useful?
Can a direct mail campaign achieve some of your objectives?
Can you get a product endorsement from a special interest group?

Price

Do you want to meet, beat or price above your competition?
Will an introductory offer work?
Will price incentives, or volume discounts serve your purposes?

These are only a few of the questions that should be asked for each of the four ps. The point is, in order to be successful, pre-planning is essential.

SALES ANALYSIS

To ignore sales analysis is like planning a moon shot, and picking a date by throwing a dart at the calendar. It can still be done – but we can't guarantee which moon you will land on. Lack of sales analysis leads to poor forecasting, which leads to poor marketing, which leads to poor sales performance, which leads to poor company performance, which leads to the unemployment line in town.

To keep abreast of the market in your territory, you must know your customers' trends, and what level of business they, and therefore you, will have in any given period. It is imperative to review sales production (by account) regularly, to see if your figures are up or down. Every salesperson is concerned when their numbers are off target with a customer and they want to find out the reasons why. The same should hold true when production figures are up. It's not good enough to notch up the extra sales to excellent work on your part (although this may be true). Sales up, or down, could mean that either you, or your competitor, has done something out of the usual. Rather than guess, it is far better to find the cause.

SALES FORECASTING

When it comes to forecasting, I have always found it best to maintain an optimistic outlook, and yet not be blind to reality. Having said this, I have always forecast my sales figures on the higher side. The reason is simple. I feel that if someone forecasts low and hits the mark, he or she hasn't really achieved much. On the other hand, if someone aims high and comes up short, at least they were still on the playing field while the low guy was in the locker room taking a shower.

How important is forecasting? In a word, *very*. It gives your organization the input it needs to figure out manning levels, (including your inside support), distribution requirements, advertising and promotion, budgets and the research and development for new or existing products that you sell. It also dictates territorial quotas and pricing policies for the upcoming period. Clearly, this is not an exercise in futility.

Forecasting isn't like pulling numbers out of a hat, or consulting the swami and his crystal ball. There are a couple of good indicators to help you along. Take a look at the National Economic Forecast and the Industry Sales Forecast. You don't have to be an economist from Oxford or Cambridge to interpret these things; they are already explained fairly well. From these you can at least see what the experts are predicting and be guided accordingly. Finally, the best reading on how good, or bad, business is likely to be, will come from your customers themselves. Ask your buyers what they are projecting. When you put these together and check them against your production figures by account, you will take a great deal of the guesswork out of forecasting.

COMPETITIVE ANALYSIS

To be truly effective in the marketing and selling of a product or service, you must know your competition almost as well as your own company. Only by knowing their strengths and weaknesses, can you stay away from the former and concentrate on the latter.

Each product is different. This is so because it is made by, serviced through and sold by way of different people in every company. If you know how your product stacks up against your competitor's, you won't have to rely on your customer's interpretation of the facts. She is sometimes misinformed!

Conversely, if she throws you off balance with a statement about your product versus brand 'x', evidently you haven't done enough home-work. You should be telling her what the differences are. If a competitor has a product feature that you can't offer, turn this around and tell the buyer about the exclusive benefits that only you can supply her. No matter what the case, if you know who and what you are selling against, you can prepare for the battle.

By now the marketing picture is pretty well focused. When we sell, we should do so with the total product in mind, which is much more than the physical product or service. It includes availability, delivery, installation, accessories, instructions, packaging, service facilities, etc. By being alert to selling opportunities, we can create competitive advantages for ourselves. For example, if your product availability is superior and your delivery times are excellent, couldn't you sell your customer on a lower inventory in his warehouse because you have what he needs in yours? A lower inventory means cost savings which translate to your company being a better buy.

Notwithstanding everything we know today about marketing, mis-takes can still be made. A major pet food company found this out the hard way. The company in question spent enormous sums of time and money developing what was slated to be the number one selling dog food in the country. Laboratory tests, blending and checks on nutri-tional values were done; nothing was left to chance. A great package and label were designed and advertising companies were geared up with a major campaign. Everything was ready. The only problem the firm had was that they couldn't sell the product – no grocer wanted to stock it. They ordered an investigation and told one of their experts to find the cause behind the super-product becoming the super-flop. After a week, a five-word report was received: 'The dogs don't like it'.

The moral of this story is simple. Always apply the latest techniques and use the best marketing and sales tools that you have, but *never* lose sight of your customer's wants and needs. Your prospect will buy what you are selling only if you are selling what he is buying!

4

Organized Selling

Confucius once said: 'In all things, success depends upon preparation, and without such preparation there is sure to be failure.' This is the theme behind the concept for organized selling – preparation. There are two things that are fairly consistent with most people. The first is that we are slaves to our habits. The second is that we can always find time for the things that we *want* to do. In selling, therefore, we should strive to make our habits good ones and resolve to make the time to prepare.

PLANNING

Every salesperson has countless responsibilities. Their territory must be well defined and organized. They must have an in-depth knowledge of each account, and this information must be properly recorded. They must be absolutely and completely familiar with not only their own product line but also that of their competition. There are reports to be filed along with other administrative duties and obligations. Finally, salespeople must plan their work and work their plan.

It is obvious that selling is no job for the timid or weak. Nor is it a job for anyone who wants to produce less than a 100 per cent effort. What it is, is a very demanding but very rewarding career.

Most, if not all salespeople, are required to file a series of reports. There are call reports, weekly itineraries, target account updates, VIP account sales figures, actual versus quota sales figures, expense accounts, etc. All of these reports must be handled along with other duties. Among these are: following up on customer requests, following up on sales proposals, following up on promises you have made, answering correspondence, sending out enquiries, complying with internal requests for information, getting orders into the system promptly, formal meetings with bosses, informal meetings with other salespeople to discuss competitive activities, passing on sales leads, and the list goes on. Oh yes, I almost forgot, you are expected to be out selling four, or four-and-a-half days per week.

No, I'm not kidding. Nor have I crossed over that fine line that places people in padded cells. There is much to do, but it can be done and done well. All it takes is proper planning. A friend of mine, 'Pistol Pete', had a great formula that was drilled into him during his stint in the US Navy. It was called the principle of the seven ps: 'Proper preparation and planning prevent piss poor performance'. Not only is performance improved through proper planning, but just as important, time is saved.

MANAGING YOUR TIME

'Time, like all things, must be managed.' Aristotle made this statement more than 2000 years ago. I think it fair to say that what was true then, is still true today. You can manage time if you go about it in a systematic way:

1. Identify your high return activities.
2. Establish priorities.
3. Start with, and concentrate on, priorities.
4. Never give up until you are finished.
5. Delegate as much as you can.
6. Never tolerate reverse delegation.
7. Allocate yourself uninterrupted time to accomplish tasks.
8. Take time to plan effectively.

These steps probably seem quite easy and simple, but they are not. I can guarantee that it will take a great deal of discipline on your part to follow these rules for time management. Why? Because, we are generally so busy we don't have the time to do these things and we certainly don't have the time to devote much thought to them either. This is a big mistake! If we make the time and take the necessary steps to plan now, we can expect a tenfold return in the future. I am not suggesting paralysis through analysis. It need not be that sophisticated nor that time-consuming. All we need is an overall plan for the month, from which a weekly plan evolves. Once you have established a weekly plan, it isn't very difficult to develop a daily plan from this. We can do this once, and do it well, provided that we make the time.

MANAGING YOUR TERRITORY

Let's begin with your territory. How do you go about managing that? It is up to you to analyse the full potential of all your accounts. Once you have done this, the high return activities can be identified and established quickly. You can then begin to concentrate on your priorities.

Next, establish short-, medium- and long-range goals for the area. Finally, you should set up a schedule for effective sales coverage.

Pre-plan a weekly itinerary. Set up target accounts. Prospect for new accounts. Spend no more time with your customer than his potential warrants (no matter how friendly he is). Now the hard part – drop any account that you feel is not worthwhile from your call cycle. They can be dealt with over the telephone.

It will help to rate your customers when analysing your territory. For example, let's say that in your business you have a few accounts who produce £500,000+ of business each year. From this point, we scale down to a large number who produce perhaps £5000 or less, each year. Let's also assume that you have 200 active accounts in the sales area that you cover. Now you can begin classifying your customers.

VIP:	£500,000 or more
A:	£250,000–£500,000
B:	£100,000–£250,000
C:	£5,000–£100,000
D:	£5,000 or less

Next, let's take a hypothetical spread for the 200 accounts:

VIP:	10
A:	20
B:	30
C:	40
D:	100

It is now quite obvious where your attention should be focused and to what degree. We should keep in mind that some accounts demand more time than others. This is not necessarily in order of account importance either. Frequently, the 'VIP' and 'A' customers only want to see you every four, six or eight weeks. On the other hand, some 'C' and 'D' accounts may want you in their office every other day. Where do you draw the line?

The answer to this lies in the call frequency outline that you should have. Everybody knows that there are 365 days in a year. However, our

working time is significantly less than that. Perhaps we should calculate
exactly how many selling days we are actually working with:

---

52 weeks available
 3 weeks personal holidays (subtract)
 2 weeks holidays (subtract: these are national holidays)
 2 weeks mis. (subtract: these are sick days, doctors, days off)

45 weeks of work

× 5 days per week

225 days

From this total, we should deduct one day per week for office time when
we set up appointments, attend sales meetings, submit reports, do
follow-ups, etc. So when we deduct a further 49 days (the holiday and
miscellaneous weeks are considered as short weeks), we are left with a
grand total of 176 selling days per year! That's it – 176. We obviously
don't have as much selling time as we may have thought, so we had best
be sure that we make at least six good calls per day. This now gives us a
total of 1,056 sales calls per year.

It is time now to go back to our account spread and see exactly how
much time we should devote to each of our customers.

VIP:	10 accounts	×	12 calls/year	=	120 calls
A:	20 accounts	×	9 calls/year	=	180 calls
B:	30 accounts	×	6 calls/year	=	180 calls
C:	40 accounts	×	4 calls/year	=	160 calls
D:	100 accounts	×	3 calls/year	=	300 calls
Total					940 calls

This leaves us with an availability of 116 calls per year to handle
customer requests for meetings, unforeseen cancellations, prospecting,
etc. In other words, you have some breathing space in your schedule.

Obviously the sample territory that I have used here won't exactly fit into everyone's framework, but it should give you some idea of how to go about setting one up. Of course you will also have to take into account your sales manager's objectives, as well as company policy. None the less, it is of paramount importance that we make the time to properly analyse our customer base, and know whose demands on our time are justified. Return on investment applies to not only stocks and bonds, but also to the hours in our days.

Stay on top of the job of updating profiles, by doing so at the end of each call (when the information is freshest). Failing this, do it no later than at the end of the day. Record the small details about your customer in a special remarks column. For example, if she likes golfing, or her daughter is studying medicine at university, or her birthday is on December 25, make a point to record these facts. You may not believe that these bits of information are important, but they can reap fantastic rewards for you. They give you a personal contact with your customer which show that you care and is light years ahead of opening comments like, 'Fine day, isn't it?'

In almost every call that you make your customer mentions something personal about him or herself. These are the first signs of developing a friendship. Although friendships should be cultivated for more than just business reasons, friendships in business do offer certain advantages. Friends don't like saying 'no' to friends. You will find that the detailing of what may seem like trivial information, can actually provide you with this significant asset. Understand the importance of your profile and recognize it for what it is – a very powerful sales tool.

The profile is also the place where the customer's business cycle is recorded. By recording your client's business cycle, you will know your own. It will also tell you when the time is right to get back in there to see her, *before* she places her next order.

Isn't it a curious thing how the same salespeople seem to thrive in good times and in bad? The lesser lights normally attribute this mysterious success to good fortune. Every salesperson has the will to succeed, but this is not enough. They also need the will to prepare.

DOUBLE YOUR CALLS – DOUBLE YOUR SALES

There have been numerous studies conducted on how the average salesperson spends his or her time. When all the different results are combined, we emerge with a picture that looks like this:

Face-to-face selling:	30 per cent
Travel:	30 per cent
Waiting to see accounts:	5 per cent
Entertaining:	6 per cent
Prospecting:	4 per cent
Writing reports:	8 per cent
Telephone work:	10 per cent
Administrative duties:	7 per cent
	100 per cent

The fact that salespeople spend precious little time actually selling is born out by these statistics. However, with proper planning and preparation, your selling time can be increased from 30 per cent to 50–60 per cent, even 75 per cent! Hard to believe isn't it. Well, I'll prove it to you.

Let's look at the average day for the average salesperson (this is the former Jack Average). Jack leaves home at 9 am and gets to his first appointment for 9.30 am. He leaves there at 10.00 am and drives for 15 minutes to meet with his 10.30 am customer. When he leaves this buyer at 11 am, he calls his office to get his messages and take care of a few details. It is now 11.15 am and he is off and running to his next appointment, which is scheduled for 11.45 am.

At 12.15 pm, when the call is finished, he suggests that he and his customer grab a fast sandwich together. At 12.45 pm, he says goodbye to this customer and heads for his car. His next meeting is not scheduled until 1.30 pm. To avoid wasting time, he spends the next 20 minutes reviewing competitive reports. It has been a good 20 minutes; he has picked up three solid leads for new business. At 1.05 pm, he drives to his customer's office and arrives there at 1.25 pm. So far, he is right on schedule.

He sees his account at 1.30 pm sharp, and leaves at 2 pm. His next appointment is a little further away and it takes him 30 minutes to get there. Jack gives himself some breathing room in his schedule today, and now has 30 minutes before he sees his next customer at 3 pm. He stays in his car and for the purposes of keeping up with his workload, he works from 2.30 pm to 3 pm doing his call reports for the morning. He enters the building at 3 pm, waits a couple of minutes to see the buyer, spends 25 minutes, and then leaves to go back to his office at 3.27 pm.

He planned his last appointment carefully so that he wasn't far away from his office. As a result, he arrives back at his desk at 3.47 pm. From 3.47 pm to 3.57 pm, he finishes his last call reports on the accounts that he saw today. Jack will now spend the next 31 minutes calling the accounts that he will see tomorrow, so that the appointments are all reconfirmed. Then, from 4.28 pm to 5 pm, he checks on orders, reviews files for the next day and writes a letter. At 5 pm he leaves his office to return to the comforts of his home, after having spent a full and conscientious day on the job.

No one can deny Jack has put in a solid day's work. Surely he has. Nor can anyone accuse him of wasting time, he hasn't. Or, has he? Jack certainly worked hard enough but did he work smart?

Let's dissect his day and see how his time was spent:

```
0900–0930: travel          =  30 minutes
0930–1000: selling         =  30 minutes
1000–1015: travel          =  15 minutes
1015–1030: waiting         =  15 minutes
1030–1100: selling         =  30 minutes
1100–1115: telephone       =  15 minutes
1115–1145: travel          =  30 minutes
1145–1215: selling         =  30 minutes
1215–1245: entertaining    =  30 minutes
1245–1305: prospecting     =  20 minutes
1305–1325: travel          =  20 minutes
1325–1330: waiting         =   5 minutes
1330–1400: selling         =  30 minutes
1400–1430: travel          =  30 minutes
1430–1500: reports         =  30 minutes
1500–1502: waiting         =   2 minutes
1502–1527: selling         =  25 minutes
1527–1547: travel          =  20 minutes
1547–1557: reports         =  10 minutes
1557–1628: telephone       =  31 minutes
1628–1700: administration  =  32 minutes
```

Now let's group the activities and see how the eight hours (480 minutes) were spent:

Selling:	145 minutes	=	30.0 per cent
Travel:	145 minutes	=	30.0 per cent
Waiting:	22 minutes	=	5.0 per cent
Entertaining:	30 minutes	=	6.0 per cent
Prospecting:	20 minutes	=	4.0 per cent
Reports:	40 minutes	=	8.0 per cent
Telephone:	46 minutes	=	10.0 per cent
Administration:	32 minutes	=	7.0 per cent
	480 minutes	=	100.0 per cent

Better planning for the day would have yielded much better results than these. There are many ways in which selling time can be maximized. Listed below are 25 suggestions:

1. Make appointments (and don't reconfirm).
2. Start early.
3. Set your priorities for the day.
4. The most important calls are morning calls – you are freshest.
5. Pre-plan your route to minimize travel time.
6. Consolidate sales calls in the same area.
7. Evaluate the necessity of each call.
8. When a telephone call will suffice, let it!
9. Prepare fully for each call.
10. Have a goal or objective for each call.
11. Don't spend too much time with the friendly account.
12. Eliminate goodwill calls.
13. Control the meeting.
14. Be on time for appointments.
15. Respect your customer's time.
16. Set up breakfast and/or luncheon meetings.
17. Know your customer's hours and when it is best to see him/her.
18. Control the time spent on lunch.
19. Eliminate unproductive breaks.
20. Capitalize on waiting time: review presentation, do reports.
21. Do your paperwork after hours.
22. Keep your reports brief and concise.
23. Minimize non-essential paperwork.
24. When out of town, stay in the area you will be working in.
25. Make use of the cellular telephone.

Through proper pre-planning, a salesperson can, and will, maximize the number of quality sales calls made every day. Keep in mind the fact that between the hours of 8 am and 6 pm, clients are available to be seen. I call these the holy hours. Reserve them for selling. Don't waste them by performing activities that can be accomplished any time.

In addition, when servicing accounts, make it your routine to have a complete sales kit on hand. Be sure to check your customer's stock before leaving your office, and don't forget to sell your entire line. Sell your product, your company and yourself (you are his or her contact; you are a problem solver; you are the best sales tool that you possess). Finally, leave a copy of your itinerary in your office, so that they know where to reach you in the event that a customer must talk to you immediately. Being reachable is a sign of being professional.

We have looked at ways of maximizing selling time. Now it is time to put these rules to the test. Let's take a look at Polly Productive who practises these time-saving techniques.

Her first appointment is with Bob Smith of Apex. They rendezvous for coffee at 8.30 am near Bob's office. For the next 40 minutes, they discuss Bob's new production line and Polly goes into detail about how her company can supply some of the key materials needed. At 9.10 am, she walks across the street to meet with DCB Industries. Between 9.15 am and 10.15 am, the negotiations are completed and Polly now drives the ten minutes to her next appointment. Once outside, she calls her office from her cellular phone and takes care of her messages between 10.25 am and 10.45 am. At 10.45 am, she meets with Titan and leaves at 11 am. She drives five minutes to her next call, and waits five minutes before she can see Mrs Jeffrey. During this five minute wait, she writes a quick note to her production people, explaining what Bob Smith needs in the way of a delivery schedule for certain parts that he is ordering. This call with Mrs Jeffrey lasts from 11.10 am to 11.45 am. She leaves her office and drives ten minutes to the restaurant. At noon, Bill Sharp arrives for their luncheon meeting.

By 1.15 pm, after discussing business and eating lunch, they part ways. Polly then drives 15 minutes to M & N Company, and sees this account from 1.30 pm to 1.55 pm. She leaves the building, crosses the street, and meets her next account at 2.00 pm. This call will be somewhat longer than usual because Jack Lang wants Polly's advice on whether certain equipment should be upgraded or changed. Once the meeting is over at 3.30 pm, she calls her office to get her afternoon messages and give instructions on certain matters. At 3.45 pm, Polly hangs up the telephone and drives 15 minutes to her last call for the day. From 4 pm to 4.45 pm, she finalizes the details for delivery to the seven

Acme facilities in the city. A quick 20-minute drive finds her back in her company parking lot.

She writes another letter and leaves both on her secretary's desk for typing tomorrow morning. She picks up the package that she asked her secretary to leave for her when they talked earlier in the day, and then leaves the office to go home at 5.30 pm.

Later that evening, when the kids are tucked up into bed, she completes her call reports for the day. Now she goes for the package that her secretary put together on her behalf. Great, everything is there. All the files on tomorrow's appointments, as well as their list of orders currently in-house; the status updates can now be reviewed. A quick check to make sure that everything is in order, and now she has some time to read competitive and trade reports. That's it! It's time to relax because tomorrow is a big day. She'll be out selling.

All right, it's report card time for Polly. How did she do with her selling time? To begin with, because she left her house prior to 9 am, we should not allocate travel time for her to get to her coffee appointment at 8.30 am. After all, the time she used before 9 am was her personal time. For the record, however, she left home this morning at 7.45 am.

0830–0910:	selling and entertaining:	=	40 minutes
0910–0915:	travel	=	5 minutes
0915–1015:	selling	=	60 minutes
1015–1025:	travel	=	10 minutes
1025–1045:	telephone	=	20 minutes
1045–1100:	selling	=	15 minutes
1100–1105:	travel	=	5 minutes
1105–1110:	report	=	5 minutes
1110–1145:	selling	=	35 minutes
1145–1155:	travel	=	10 minutes
1155–1200:	waiting	=	5 minutes
1200–1315:	selling and entertaining	=	75 minutes
1315–1330:	travel	=	15 minutes
1330–1355:	selling	=	25 minutes
1355–1400:	travel	=	5 minutes
1400–1530:	selling	=	90 minutes
1530–1545:	telephone	=	15 minutes
1545–1600:	travel	=	15 minutes
1600–1645:	selling	=	45 minutes
1645–1705:	travel	=	15 minutes

For the purposes of calculating and comparing her time with Jack Average's, the clock stops at 5 pm. The additional 25 minutes that she spent in the office, again do not count as this was personal time.

Let's take a look at how Polly spent her time today and check the percentages for each activity.

Selling:	385 minutes	=	62.0 per cent
Travel:	80 minutes	=	13.0 per cent
Waiting:	5 minutes	=	0.5 per cent
Entertaining:	115 minutes	=	18.0 per cent*
Prospecting:	0 minutes	=	0.0 per cent
(done at home in the evening)			
Reports:	5 minutes	=	0.5 per cent
(majority done after hours)			
Telephone:	35 minutes	=	6.0 per cent
Administration:	0 minutes	=	0.0 per cent
(done after hours)			
	625 minutes	=	100.0 per cent

(*Although Polly was selling at breakfast and lunch, she was also entertaining.)

According to these figures, Polly was actually working an extra 145 minutes in her day versus Jack. Some may argue, however, that 115 minutes should not be allocated to both selling and entertaining. It should be one or the other. OK, let's knock off the entertaining time because this was fundamentally selling time. We will consider the entertaining part as being a bonus. We are now left with the same amount of selling time, 385 minutes. However, the selling percentage should be calculated against a total of 510 minutes for the day. This equates to *75 per cent* of face-to-face customer contact! This is a far cry from today's average of 30 per cent.

There are probably more than just a few sceptics who might want to question the reality of actually maintaining a schedule like Polly's. The scepticism is justified; there aren't very many Pollys out there. However, if we talk to the top salespeople we know, and ask them what their routine is like, chances are we will get a similar description for their day.

Why do these salespeople do so well? It is a combination of working smart and keeping the law of averages on their side. It is only logical that the more sales calls they make, the more sales they make. They don't get caught up with the stigma of the 80/20 rule: 80 per cent of the time being spent with 20 per cent of the business base. This leads nowhere in sales. We come to realize from these examples that our time must be based on a return on our investment.

One final point should be made before closing this section. Always have safety valves in your schedule to allow for the unexpected. The unexpected can be: the customer who must see you today; a sales call lasting longer than anticipated; or any other of a number of possible events.

When we look back at Jack Average's schedule, we see a fairly consistent 30 minutes or so spent with each account. Polly's meetings, on the other hand, carried on for a period of between 15 and 90 minutes. When she made her appointments, she set them for general times, like mid-morning, late afternoon, etc. Her only exceptions to this rule were her breakfast and luncheon meetings, and her Titan visit at 10.45 am. The Titan purchasing manager was running on an extremely tight schedule and could only see her then for 15 minutes.

Polly was also allowing for unexpected events because her 4 pm meeting could have been delayed. She knew Monica Lloyd at Acme well enough to see her after 5 pm because she is always in the office until 7 pm. Conversely, she could have postponed the meeting until the following day if absolutely necessary; she could make room in her schedule then. This means, essentially, that Polly was available to handle emergencies after 3.30 pm when she finished up with Jack Lang. She really did plan her day well, after all.

Suffice it to say, this kind of planning takes time as well as a thorough knowledge of the territory and accounts. As we saw from Polly's example, she used her personal time for the greatest portion of her travel and she used her personal time for planning. She also used her personal time for administrative duties, reports and prospecting. It would appear that Polly used her personal time to invest in her career.

5

Details and Impressions

APPEARANCES

The way we as salespeople dress has a profound effect on how people view and treat us. As an example of this, it is generally accepted that prospective employers can be seriously discouraged from hiring an applicant who comes to an interview either over- or underdressed. There is a way to dress for leisure and a definite way to dress for business.

Clothing should be selected and worn as a sales tool. Efficiency and effectiveness are far more important than aesthetics. We will always encounter some accounts that prefer stylish and/or eccentric dressers; most times, however, a smart, neat and tailored look projects a more professional image. John Molloy, in his book *Dress for Success*, clearly illustrates this point. Mr Molloy conducted exhaustive research on the subject of what to wear, when to wear it and the effect that wearing it has on our prospects. He has come up with some very interesting conclusions.

For example, a solid suit gives you a more genial appearance than pinstripes; pinstripes transmit an imposing image. In addition, upper middle-class people tend to be more attracted to a salesperson wearing a grey suit; the lower middle class prefer a blue outfit. Another intriguing point that he makes has to do with our conditioning. Anyone wearing clothing associated with the upper middle class will generally be assumed to belong to this group. In other words, if we look the part, we assume the part. Obviously, as salespeople the clothes we wear can contribute enormously to the overall effect we have on our customers.

Another example is that a black suit suggests a very authoritative nature. In fact, black suits should rarely be worn for that very reason. There is such a thing as overpowering people! A rule of the thumb is that the darker the suit, the more authoritative the individual.

If you are already naturally authoritative looking and want to negate this, wearing lighter shades of blue, grey or beige can accomplish your goal. Furthermore, people instinctively feel more comfortable with, and less threatened by, someone wearing a light grey or light blue solid. You may find that people warm up to you more quickly and easily when wearing these colours.

Choosing an outfit, using forethought based on who you are seeing, is obviously a necessity. When selling to women, men should avoid soft colours. This is definitely not the type of image that he will want to transmit.

Purchasing agents from a low- to a middle-class background, prefer salespeople wearing conservative clothing; no power/authoritative type clothing should be worn here. On the other hand, a purchasing agent from a middle- to upper-class background will be better impressed by this authoritative attire.

When clothing suggestions conflict for the clients you will be seeing on a particular day, the order of importance regarding what to wear is: occupation, then location (office, project site).

When out buying business clothing, you are in a very enviable position. You are the customer! Insist on service and do not allow your salesperson to intimidate you. Buy only what you want and settle for nothing less. If you can't find exactly what you are looking for in the shop, shop elsewhere. You don't have to compromise, so why do it? The clothing business is no different from your own. There are a lot of competitors out there just waiting for a chance to sell you what you need, or don't need in some cases.

Walking into a clothing store these days, can be like going on an odyssey with Alice in Wonderland. You have before you colours, shapes, patterns, designs, sizes, styles and fabrics. Decisions, decisions! I have always followed one credo, however, which has helped enormously when buying any wearing apparel: buy quality.

The same rule applies to dress shirts. Quality speaks for itself. As for colour, and contrary to what some may believe, white is still by far the best colour for business. If, on occasion, you feel an absolute need for a coloured blouse or shirt, stay with a solid and preferably a blue. Remember what was said earlier about the upper middle class? Studies have indicated that the subtle and paler shades of shirting are most synonymous with this group. Never wear short sleeves to see a customer, unless you are either in a tropical climate, or it is the general custom for the area you are working in. Lastly, you are better to break a dress rule, rather than make a customer feel that either you or he is out of place.

The same can be said about a necktie for a man. In some countries where I have sold, to wear a necktie would arouse suspicion. We have to temper normal convention with common sense. Ordinarily, however, a tie represents much more than a piece of fabric tied around a man's neck. In many ways it is status symbol. It distinguishes between white- and blue-collar male workers in America, Europe and most parts of Asia. It is an important piece of clothing that should be selected with as much care as a suit.

For our male readers, the easiest way to buy the right tie, is to perform this ritual at the same time as you buy a suit. You can co-ordinate them, with the help of the salesperson perhaps, right there on the spot. If you don't take care of this detail then, you can be almost guaranteed frustration and aggravation later when you are trying to get the right look.

Neckties then are extremely important in bringing the total outfit together. Men should neither wear anything gaudy, nor anything unusual in colour nor design. When wearing a tie with a striped design, you should work at getting the stripes to meet at right angles when the knot at the neck is tied. Be sure to get the length level with your belt buckle. The best suit and shirt combination will look rotten if it doesn't harmonize well. Give this aspect of your outfit the attention it deserves.

Now that we are dressed from top to toe (almost), it is time to mention shoes. Shoes should of course, match the outfit of the day. Black, brown and cordovan will always co-ordinate well with anything in your wardrobe. A quick point to remember about shoes is that if they aren't shining, then neither are you. A £1000 suit of clothes, accompanied by scruffy shoes, looks scruffy.

Well, we are just about ready to make our assault on the business world. There are only a few items left to think about. First, the haircut. Today, it is not essential that you walk around with the forties look – women's hair tied back and men's hair short and off the ears and collar. In any experiments that I have been involved with, however, multi-coloured, spiked or very long hair still hasn't gained much acceptance with most business people. The shorter and neater hair styles are still preferred by our prospects. The same holds true for men's facial hair. It is neater and better, not to have any when selling. Seldom will facial hair enhance a man's appearance. The only exception to this rule is on those occasions when a special effect is sought: you either want to look older, or are trying to hide a weak chin. Otherwise, the clean-cut, clean-shaven look will work best.

Next come the accessories – the finishing touches. Always buy the best that you can afford. This applies to watches, wallets, belts, pens, pads, folders, briefcases, etc. People really do notice. A great looking outfit can be overshadowed by a salesperson walking in with a 29 pence pen and a weather beaten briefcase. (I've seen some salespeople walk into an office with a carrier bag attached to their wrist . . . honest!)

Nothing can break the good looking image faster than forgetting the details. If we have smart looking accessories to match our outfit, it is good for our attitude. If we look good, we feel good.

Last, but certainly not least, comes jewellery. This is not to be confused with accessories; it is entirely different. Women should wear tasteful and *functional* jewellery, and even then not much of it. Men should avoid it altogether. (There are some individuals, including customers, who have odd notions about men who wear jewellery.) As salespeople, we have enough legitimate work ahead of us in a normal day, without adding unnecessarily to the effort.

DOS AND DON'TS

In concluding this section on appearance, I have outlined a ready reference list of the dos and don'ts involved in proper dress attire. Remember, your aim is to look how your customer wants you to look.

DO

- ensure that a man's shirt is lighter than his outfit;
- ensure that the necktie is darker than the shirt;
- dress affluently when there is a choice;
- always be clean (including fingernails);
- dress as well as the people that you are selling to;
- carry a good attaché case and pen and pencil set; and
- check in the mirror before seeing a customer.

DON'T

- wear two different patterns together;
- wear jewellery that is not functional;
- men shouldn't wear any item which may be considered effeminate;
- wear items which may identify a personal association or belief;
- wear sunglasses when facing a customer;
- remove your jacket unless you must;
- wear gels or creams that give your hair a greasy look; and
- wear green (unless you are Irish and it's St Patrick's Day).

When you aren't sure what type of selling situation you are likely to have on a certain day, you should dress more conservatively than normal. Also, to avoid a last minute outfit, which may or may not be suitable for the day, I recommend that you select and lay out your clothes the night before. Once you have developed a pattern of dressing right for the right occasion, you may wish to chart your selling successes against the type of clothing you were wearing. The results may amaze you. You can dress for success!

FIRST IMPRESSIONS

Without a doubt, first impressions are among the most important aspects of selling. During the first 60 seconds spent with your prospects, they are making up their mind whether they will listen (not only hear, but actually listen) to your story, and whether or not they are going to believe what you have to say. In other words, your buyers are deciding if you have a chance to sell or not.

If you doubt this fact, all that you have to do is go to your nearest library and sift through the mounds of material on human psychology. Believe me, you have only 60 seconds to open that sales door. Remember, you will never get a second chance to make your first impression!

Fortunately, you can control this aspect of your first encounter in a variety of ways. For example, as mentioned, your appearance plays a large part. Are you dressed properly to meet this individual? Do your opening words convey sincerity? Do you display confidence by the way you enter your prospect's office. Is your handshake firm and is your smile genuine? All of these factors contribute to the judgement your client intuitively makes about you.

Factors which you may consider to be inconsequential can turn the account against you. Negative impressions can be created by shopworn samples, dog-eared flyers, sloppy appointment books, disorganized notes and all of your personal accessories.

Think and plan ahead for the people that you will be seeing, taking into account where you will be seeing them. It is obvious that you should try to plan your calls for any given day with the same class or type of account. Make your first impression the right and lasting one.

6
Customer Perceptions

REMEMBERING NAMES

As a professional salesperson, the importance of remembering names cannot be overly stressed. It shows that you are genuinely interested in others and that your customer is an important person to you, in or out of his office.

There is no magic formula to help in remembering names. The process itself is a relatively simple one, all it takes is effort and practice. To begin with, when you meet someone for the first time, you should never think of what you are going to say or do after the introduction. This alone is probably the major reason why we forget a name – we never heard it in the first place. Instead of thinking ahead, concentrate on the individual you are seeing, because you have never seen him before. Scrutinize the physical characteristics of this person and get a very clear impression of what he looks like. Next, listen carefully to the name itself. If you didn't get it properly registered, ask for it to be repeated. On the second occasion, whoever is making the introduction, will make a greater effort to give you a better articulated version.

What if you still haven't got it after the second attempt? Ask for the spelling. Don't be shy about doing this. In fact, most people will be flattered by your insistence on getting their name right. Now that you have finally registered the moniker correctly, begin to use it frequently. There is no need to be gushy, but it is a good idea to use his name as often as the situation warrants. The more you use it, the more deeply registered it becomes.

Next, and this is a very important step, try to make an association between the person and the name. For example, if you meet a Miss Shorter, it is obvious that you will make a connection between this girl's name and height. Or if you are lucky enough to meet a dentist called Dr Gumb, you can not only make the relationship for his name, but also his profession.

SELF-IMPROVEMENT

There are a number of ways in which we can continually improve. Good manners, for example, are often taken for granted, but never should be. It would be a good idea to buy a book on etiquette, and read it. Nothing can destroy a favourable impression faster than a display of bad form. Quite frankly, there are just too many ways that we can commit a major gaffe with a customer to enumerate here. *Faux pas* ranging from sitting before being asked, chewing gum, bad table manners, etc, can all leave a bad taste in the mouth of someone who knows better. Suffice to say, that the money spent on a handbook of etiquette wouldn't be wasted.

Another area that can immediately create a good or bad impression, lies in an individual's lexicon. The standard of our vocabulary should always be on the same level as that of our customer. This can range from anything like a grunt, to the eloquence of a Winston Churchill. Few of us have any problems with lowering the level of our speech, but we should not be caught with an inability to raise it up to the standards of some of our better educated accounts. We must use words as an ally.

The easiest way to improve your word power is through wide and varied reading. You should acquire the habit of consulting a dictionary when coming across a word that you don't know. In doing this you will find your range of vocabulary increasing at an astonishing rate. Also, by reading more, you are able to pick up the meaning of unfamiliar words very often simply by seeing the context in which they are used. Once the meaning of a new word has been learned, you should use it quickly and as frequently as possible, to ensure that it becomes permanently entered into your word bank (in much the same way as a name).

Aside from the fact that more reading helps to improve our vocabulary, there is a second incentive – more general knowledge. When we see our prospect, the main business is, of course, business; however, when we get a chance to discuss more important topics than the weather (while relaxing the account) we should do so. After all, we are also being given an opportunity to know this person better. Let's face it, if you have 200 customers in your territory, you probably have 200 different personal interests. By keeping up on current affairs, your chances of discussing a subject of mutual interest are greatly enhanced.

One final note on the subject of words should include the message that anything we say must always be delivered with proper clarity, speed and pronunciation. Regardless of how extensive a vocabulary we may possess, or how widely read we are, we must express ourselves well. Anyone having a problem in this area should not get discouraged.

Eloquent speakers aren't born that way; they practise the art. As is the case in all things, perfect practice makes perfect.

SELF-IMAGE PSYCHOLOGY

'The man who believes he can do something is probably right, and so is the man who believes he can't.' This anonymous quotation holds a great deal of meaning for all of us. We have to believe in ourselves and our goals. The power of this positive thinking can frequently mean the difference between success and failure.

HW Arnold once said that, 'the worst bankrupt in the world is the person who has lost his enthusiasm.' Of all the professions, sales is the one in which we can least afford this bankruptcy. We are the ones who have to fan the flames of desire within our customer and perk up his spirits if he is down. The reverse does not hold true. When we are dispirited, we are the ones who have to pull ourselves up by our bootstraps and shake off whatever is bothering us.

I have always found it helpful to picture my better moments, and focus on these, when I am not in top form. This can do a lot to improve a self-image. Stop thinking about yourself and your problems. Try to concentrate on other individuals and devote your energies to someone else's needs. This can have a twofold benefit. First, you end up by helping someone, and second, by helping others you feel good about yourself. It really does work, and both you and your customer come out ahead.

It may not always be easy to win, but it is light years ahead of losing. To consistently win, all you have to do is work with ten basic ingredients that produce the right formula:

1. Expect to win.
2. Motivate yourself.
3. Create a positive image.
4. Be aware of your strengths and weaknesses.
5. Possess self-esteem.
6. Project yourself and your image, positively.
7. Plan your work and work your plan.
8. Resolve to achieve your goals.
9. Practise self-discipline.
10. Learn from the past, then plan for the future.

Each of us is in control of our own destiny and only we have the power to make it good or bad. It is useless to blame others for our setbacks.

When shoulders take their full responsibility, there is rarely space left over for a chip. Whatever happens to us, it is ultimately our personal responsibility – win or lose.

WHY CUSTOMERS BUY OR DON'T BUY

There are two rules:

> Rule 1: People like to buy things.
> Rule 2: People do not like to be sold.

A contradiction? No, not really. We all like to buy because of the enjoyment that we derive from having something new. The reason people don't like to be sold, is simply that we are all afraid of making a mistake. No one likes to squander hard-earned money. When it is personal money that we squander, it is disappointing; when it is corporate money, it can be disastrous if not job threatening. Therefore, it is up to the salesperson to lead the prospect in such a way, that the comfortable decision to buy can be taken.

People buy for different reasons:

- pride and prestige;
- comfort and convenience;
- safety and security;
- gain; or
- fear of loss.

The first four reasons are pretty well self-explanatory. The last, 'fear of loss', is simple to explain. Prospects fear that they may miss a chance or overlook an opportunity.

Equally, people do *not* buy for different reasons:

- fear (of making a decision);
- they already feel satisfied;
- suspicion;
- inability to make the decision;
- pride; or
- friends.

In short, people need a motivation to buy. Abraham Maslow conducted an in-depth study on human motivation and developed a list of motivational needs for people. These are:

1. physiological needs: food and water;
2. safety needs: security and protection;

3.   love needs: affection and belonging;
4.   esteem needs: self-respect and achievment; and
5.   self-actualization need: desire for self-fulfilment.

Assuming that in our society the basic needs of one through three have already been achieved and satisfied, we on a sales level are left with numbers four and five to deal with. These can be further defined as the buyer's personal needs. They are:

- recognition;
- security;
- avoiding criticism;
- self-satisfaction;
- saving time;
- making the job easier; and
- avoiding worry.

In anyone's profession, the greatest single motivation is having pride in one's work; that is, pride in what the individual has accomplished. This motivation is based on a subjective assessment, which is emotional! When we think about it, all the motivational aspects revolve around emotion. Emotion must be dealt with in customer relations because it is the single largest ingredient involved in selling. I am not suggesting that we all run down to our community college and enroll in psychology courses, but neither should we be blind to this fundamental facet of dealing with people. Being aware is half the solution to your success.

CUSTOMER JUDGEMENTS

Since the buyer's emotions are so important, it is quite reasonable to assume that her judgements about us are going to affect how she deals with us, if at all.

As a salesperson, you can expect to be judged on many things, such as:

- condition of your car;
- personal grooming;
- condition of your records, briefcase, literature, samples;
- knowledge of the customer's needs;
- being on time;
- respect for secretaries and receptionists;
- sales presentation;
- enthusiasm and sincerity;

- anticipating and overcoming objections;
- confidence in your product;
- listening habits;
- staying too long or talking too much;
- politeness and courtesy; and
- showing appreciation for the order.

In all probability, everything that has been written up to now on customer attitudes, seems to indicate that we are dealing with a very complex subject, and we are. But we deal with these complexities every day of our lives without knowing it, almost like breathing. Acknowledge that you are dealing with real people who have real emotions, and never lose sight of this fact. Instead, use this knowledge to your own advantage.

CUSTOMER CHARACTER

Before you get into your customer's office, you may sometimes gain valuable clues about his personality. Some may be as simple as hearing his name spoken by people who know him. We grow up with a name that either sticks or gets altered, depending upon how we behave. For example, what type of individuals do you imagine go by the following names: Frederick, Freddie, Fred; Elizabeth, Liz, Bethie, Beth. Amazing, but we are how we are called. Nicknames are also priceless. If a nickname stuck from childhood through adulthood, then it is a bona fide character sign.

When you enter someone's office for the first time, take a few brief seconds to look around and understand the character of the person you are about to deal with. The signs are all there and are as plain as the words in this book, if you take the time to read them. People bring a great deal of their personal lives into their offices, to give them that extra sense of security. A bowling trophy, a family portrait, a diploma, a Persian rug, or any number of things, can give you significant insights into a personality. By observing, we are able to draw some pretty accurate conclusions as to who an individual is, what his interests are and how he can be sold.

Once you begin talking to your prospect, you can quickly identify whether she has a positive or a negative disposition. This is fairly easy to achieve by listening to her choice of words. Adjust your sales approach accordingly. If she is very positive, simply be yourself. If, on the other hand, you discover that she is quite negative, do not get unnecessarily enthusiastic in your sales talk at the very beginning. Take each of your points separately and analytically, so that you build her positive reaction with each segment of your presentation. If you have done this well, her basic negativity will become overshadowed by a more positive reaction. When it comes time to close, she will be in the proper frame of mind.

CUSTOMER ATTITUDES

Remember, all people play games and the onus is on the salesperson to understand this and use it to his or her own advantage. The prospect who says, 'you can't trust anyone these days', doesn't mean that he intends to avoid people because he is afraid of 'being fleeced'. In fact, the contrary is true. What he will do is go out of his way to have more contact with people so that he will be able to reinforce his belief.

The prospect will tend to receive messages which can be expected to confirm his attitude. He will unconsciously distort, reject, or fail to hear points of disagreement. In other words, a buyer will only hear what he wants to hear, see what he wants to see and conveniently forget any part of the message which conflicts with his preconceived notions. This selective perception is difficult to overcome, but it is by no means impossible.

First, tackle a minor point on which the prospect doesn't seem to have any strong feelings and gain acceptance on that point. Continue the process of dealing with minor points and continue gaining his acceptance; eventually the buyer's defensive mechanism will be neutralized. Once this happens, new information can be introduced to an open mind. When you know the prospect well enough to predict how he will react to various messages, you can plan a more effective sales presentation.

You can see that good salesmanship requires a knowledge of not only your customer's company, but of even greater importance, the customer himself. To capture and hold your prospect's attention, an understanding of his attitude, position, experience and interests is vital. The customer wants to feel important. By listening courteously, paying attention to him and relating to his interests (family, hobbies, etc), you can achieve this and place your customer in a frame of mind to listen to you and to hear what you have to say.

As a professional, you will not only want to know the type of character you are dealing with, but also her reference group. This group supplies her with the ethics and principles that she applies to her daily life – it could be the Church, Red Cross, PTA or any number of associations. If we know what her group stands for, we know what she stands for.

One final note on customer attitudes deals with perceptions. Perceptions are among the most critical skills that you must have in order to succeed. You should always bear in mind what the customer is buying, not what you are selling. Is a Rolls-Royce buyer purchasing basic transportation or prestige? Is he buying a product or a benefit?

My favourite story, and one that best illustrates this point, is about a fellow who went from one DIY store to the next, asking for information about two-inch drills. In each store that he went into, the sales clerks told him all about the 'long-life drill motor, reversing capabilities, five-year guarantees', etc. Finally, he went into the last store and discovered a salesperson who found out not only what he wanted, a two-inch drill, but also exactly what he wanted it for. The salesperson gave the buyer a full explanation on how perfectly his drill would pierce concrete or wooden structures without leaving jagged edges. Then he showed the prospect a complete line of his drill bits. The buyer bought. What did this salesperson understand that the others did not? Simple. The buyer really wasn't buying a two-inch drill at all. He was buying a two-inch hole in his basement wall, so that he could install a heavy duty rack. The drill was merely a means of accomplishing this.

7

Alternate Sales Methods and Control Factors

TELEMARKETING

According to past studies conducted by the Rockefeller Institute in Pittsburgh, the vast majority of customers who stopped buying from regular suppliers, did so in the belief that they were being neglected. As understandable as this action is, it is equally understandable to realize that the situation could have been avoided through telephone contact.

Almost everyone today is aware of the tremendous costs involved in personal selling. The cost of making a sales call is only going in one direction – up. The fact is, there may be many accounts in your territory who don't provide you with a reasonable return on the investment of your face-to-face selling time. What do you do with these customers? Drop them? Emphatically no! They are most likely *less than marginal* accounts for your competitors as well. We are also probably safe in assuming that your competition is neglecting them. Solution: make your sales calls by telephone.

The telephone – your telephone – is a primary sales tool. It can increase your sales contacts, and therefore your productivity, significantly. Try to allocate a certain amount of time every week to telephoning so that you can stay in touch with your small and/or remote customers. This is easier than you may think. If you have a well organized customer card file, go ahead and set up a customer contact rotation system.

Once you have done this, you can then make your individual customer contacts on a weekly, bi-weekly, monthly or even quarterly basis. Establish a list of telephone accounts in the same way as you did for your active base accounts – VIP through D. Then, by using a rotating system, you could make the contacts that need to be made without neglecting anyone.

Another valuable telephone habit is the pre-qualifying of accounts. Why spend your time making a special trip to see a prospect who offers no potential for you or your company? Why indeed, when a simple telephone call could have accomplished the same thing? Learn to be an effective telemarketer.

Telemarketing, or T/M, involves much more than placing a call through to someone. It should in fact be treated with the same degree of preparation as a personal visit. If you don't want to sound like a dolt in your customer's office due to lack of preparation, you certainly don't want to sound like a dolt on the telephone for the same reason. Before calling a client, organize your thoughts by jotting points down on a piece of paper. Prepare your replies to anticipated objections. Plan a systematic presentation. Among other things, you should have the following information in front of you: customer profile, last order placed, pound amount, complaints, if any, etc. Then psyche yourself up.

You may believe that psyching yourself up for a phone call may be exaggerating the point a little, but it is just as important and worthwhile as it is when you make a face-to-face visit. Psyching affects your mood and attitude. It doesn't matter one iota whether you are sitting in a prospect's office or your own; mood and attitude are inflected through your voice. Your voice will tell your customer how enthusiastic you are about this presentation. This is obviously even truer in T/M; all your customers can 'see' is your voice. Let it be a smiling one.

In T/M, the first ten to fifteen seconds are crucial. You must identify yourself and your company, and call the person you are talking to by his or her name. Your opening statement should create interest and get your prospect involved. For example: 'Mrs Jones, my products have been proven to save companies such as yours "x" per cent over its lifetime versus what you are currently using.' Establish a rapport by being interested and informed about her business. Ask open-ended questions and point out your product benefits. When the time is right, ask for the business. Treat this call as you would a sales call made in person.

When you are making a T/M call, avoid situations that set you up for a 'no' reply. For instance, a presentation given in a monotone will indicate boredom or indifference on your part. An upward voice inflection however, will give your customer a sense of enthusiasm. Speaking too quickly suggests impatience or nervousness.

It also pays to read the other person's voice and respond accordingly. If he tries to brush you off, have a ready list of benefits and reasons to give him for hearing you out. Explain your company history and policies to reassure the prospect that you are not a 'fly-by-night' operator. Above all, do not give up.

Make a point of knowing the best time of day to contact each customer. Is she more receptive in the morning or the afternoon? If you get someone on the line who appears to be busy or distracted, arrange to call her back at a more suitable time. In this respect, avoid calling just before lunch or at the close of business.

After you have made the sale and delivered the product, call the account to thank her for the order and ensure that she is satisfied. The few minutes that it takes demonstrates more about you to the customer than you may believe imaginable. You are building a professional image.

It is not always easy though. You may actually find that you have two hurdles to overcome rather than one. You are prepared for the customer, but how about the screener? Before you accomplish anything on this call, you will have to convince the screener that your call deserves to be put through to the boss. Screeners have the power to slam the door in your face or welcome you into the office. They must be dealt with professionally.

First of all, treat them with respect. Ask for their name and then write it down on your customer profile card, so you can use it on your next call. Be an important person. If the boss is busy, give the screener two or three alternative times when you will have a chance to call back. Explain why you are important. For instance, your product may have saved similar companies thousands of pounds, or you may have a major product advancement to describe to the boss. Answer the screener's questions politely and never lie to them about the nature of the call. Telling the screener that you are calling from the centre for disease control with the boss's test results may get you through on this occasion, but it is unlikely to succeed a second time.

DIRECT MAIL

Direct mail is another way to reach a maximum number of accounts with a minimnum of time invested. If you go this route, it is important that you make your proposition or offer as attractive as you can afford to. Offer something that is free: an estimate or survey (if applicable), free brochures, free catalogues – free something! Your giveaway doesn't have to cost much, but it may still generate the interest that you are looking for.

Limited-time offers can also be very effective. They imply that what you are currently offering is special and, as such, cannot be extended beyond a certain date. If someone is even mildly interested in your product, this type of offer is bound to inspire some sort of response from him. No one wants to pass up the chance of cashing in on a good deal. (Remember Maslow's 'fear of loss'.)

There are a number of situations that may warrant a direct mail campaign. For instance, you may wish to send out a mailing to once active accounts who stopped buying from your company some time ago. Or, you may get your hands on a mailing list from a name broker or trade publication. These lists can be invaluable. They can be a start for your successful prospecting of new accounts.

PROSPECTING

Finding prospects can be very difficult, but it can also be very rewarding, both financially as well as personally. It takes a lot of determination because there are other things that you could be doing. It also demands tenacity on your part because most of the names that you come across will lead to nothing. Finally, it requires good old fashioned sleuthing. Generally you are not looking at a household name. These companies can be pretty obscure.

Where do you find these barnacle encrusted jewels? To begin with, there are name brokers and trade publications. A trade publication will often sell you their mailing list for a small fee. You also have the yellow pages from your phone book. Call various trade associations to get either their membership list or names of prospects that may be interested in your company. You can also ask your vendors for help in this area.

Other sources for prospecting include: your old customer files, newspapers, trade announcements, trade shows and your current customers. If your customer has been well sold and is satisfied with your products, she won't hesitate to suggest other companies with similar needs. Finally there is you. Be alert. Use your eyes and ears.

When you do come across the name of a prospect, make sure that you pre-qualify it before actually making a personal visit. Give yourself a quota for the number of qualified prospects that you will follow up every week. Let's face it, if you don't make an effort to open new accounts and expand your customer base, you can't expect your territory to be producing up to its potential – nor you to yours.

CONTROL (AKA TAKING CHARGE)

How does a football team win games? Ball control! How does a skier win a race? Ski control! How do top sales people win sales? Sales control! The sales profession is similar to professional sports in many ways, from practice through execution. Control plays a major part in this success.

If you as an individual want to accomplish something, you must control the events leading up to your goal. You have to call the shots. How can you hope to succeed if other people are directing your actions? Serendipity does have its limitations! Make no mistake about it, it is the responsibility of the salesperson to control the sales meeting.

The control factors begin from the moment that you call to set up a meeting. You select a time and ensure that the location is conducive to having your presentation heard without distractions or interruptions. Small talk is limited, so that you neither waste your time nor your client's.

We have already reviewed the significance of your prospect's frame of mind. There is no need to repeat the importance of getting her mind off things in general and onto your thing in particular. In addition, your presentation should be smooth and orderly, and your handling of objections must be thorough. Although many of these points will be covered later, there are, however, subtleties that should be dealt with here. They can contribute enormously to the overall effect you and your presentation have on the account.

To begin with, the way in which you enter her office has a major effect. You should smartly approach her to shake hands, displaying a complete air of confidence. Also, make a point of placing your business cards in one of your pockets so that when you reach in to take one out, it is handed to the prospect the way in which it is supposed to be read. Trivial maybe, but definitely effective.

Sales literature can be a tremendous tool when used properly. It can answer many questions before they are asked and provide visual proof of what it is you are selling. Make sure that you are the one holding this tool – I mean physically holding it! There is nothing worse than handing your prospect something to read and then sitting back in your chair watching her read it. After all, if a salesperson hands a brochure to a prospect in the middle of a presentation, what does he or she expect the prospect to do with it – use it as a coaster for a coffee mug? No. Generally the account will feel compelled to review it, there and then. So don't make this mistake. When you clutch your literature in that vice-like grip of yours, you can show your client what you want her to see, when you want her to see it. What is more important, it also draws her closer to you.

While you are writing things out for your account (including her order), it is wise to avoid using a red pen. We are so conditioned, all of us, that red gets naturally interpreted as meaning *stop*. This is not what we want to see happen here. Save the red for the home or office when you get an urge to doodle.

One final note here is appropriate: that is about how to handle promotional items, 'giveaways'. There are countless millions of corporate pounds wasted every year on giveaways because they seem to be given away as an afterthought, or as an obligation to get rid of the thing. It boggles the mind that so much money can be spent on such a valuable tool, with so little direction on how to properly use the device.

Too many times, I have seen a salesperson reaching into his or her briefcase and pulling out an array of merchandise that would make Santa envious at Christmas; and unceremoniously hand their prospect one of these and two of those. It doesn't even seem to matter whether he or she is doing business with this company or not. Personally, I would never give a gift to an individual that I am not doing business with. Call it a principle. I feel that this gesture can be improperly construed as some kind of payoff in the hopes of getting a return later.

To achieve the fullest benefit from your giveaways requires nothing more than common sense. Tell your account that you have brought her something from your office that you thought she might enjoy, need, appreciate or use. The point is that you want her to realize that you were thinking of her in particular. It is the small things that count and which are remembered.

ENTERTAINMENT

Most of the rules for entertaining involve simple common sense too. Basically they can be qualified in a few points:

1. Entertainment should be business related.
2. A business discussion should take place during this period.
3. It should follow norms, practices and policies of your company.
4. The setting should be conducive to a business discussion.
5. It should be appropriate for the individual that you are with.
6. It should provide a return on investment.

What do you do with a very important customer who prefers to drink lunch instead of eating it? This is a sensitive issue, but it can be overcome. First, never invite a luncheon guest who you know is going to try to turn a normal lunch into a drinking marathon. You certainly don't have the time for it, even if he does. Second, if entertaining a drinker is unavoidable, do so outside normal business hours and don't try to keep pace with him. Make sure that you have an escape by telling him, just after you get together, that you have to be somewhere else at a certain time. Once all of these precautions have been taken, go ahead and enjoy yourself. Again, this comes down to the simple rule of knowing your accounts well enough to select the appropriate entertainment for each.

Perhaps the greatest advantage in entertaining a customer comes from the opportunity both you and he have of really getting to know one another. What a plus for you personally, and for your company in general! A gentleman that I once knew put it crudely, but succinctly, when he said, 'hell boy, when you get to know your customer well, you become friends; friends hate to refuse friends.' He was, of course, referring to asking for business – and it's true. This is not to say that your sole purpose in entertaining customers should be to set up a temporary ruse whereby you get a temporary gain. The business gain is actually a bi-product of the friendship received.

I have also had customers of mine take me out at their expense. Now, some may question the logic in letting a customer pick up the bill, but I believe it makes abundant sense. There is no better way of telling you that he likes you for you, and not just for the company that you represent. Besides, he may very well be offended if, because of your business relationship, you never allow him to pay the bill. He may think that what *he* took as being a friendship, *you* took as being strictly business.

8
Negotiating

TECHNIQUES

Negotiation in selling is as much a fact of life as are death and taxes. The age old question is: 'Are you giving away more than you have to?'

Because of the importance of this chapter, I have broken it down into two categories: Negotiating Techniques; and Negotiating Price. Although some of the techniques described in this section may not be appropriate or desirable in your customer dealings, they are none the less important. You need a basic understanding of negotiating *before* you can properly negotiate price. For this reason, we will go through some of the fundamentals here which will help you later. In any event, these negotiating techniques can, and will, be of assistance the next time that you are out buying something for yourself.

In negotiating, contrary to popular belief, you should never be out to try to 'screw' the other guy. In fact, what you should be attempting to achieve is a 'win-win' situation for both you and your adversary. Some quick points are:

- build trust;
- show trust;
- keep your word;
- try a different approach to problems if positions become rigid;
- take the 'nice guy' approach;
- genuinely understand the other person's position;
- accept style as more important than substance; and
- be nonchalant.

This last point may give you the impression that I am suggesting that you take negotiating lightly. This isn't the case. What I mean here, is that you should give your opponent the impression that the outcome is no big deal to you one way or the other. It is important, but not that important. If you can't strike a deal, it is not the end of the world; you have other fish to fry. If he is made to believe that these negotiations are more important to him than they are to you, he is also likely to commit to making the first concession.

Unfortunately, not everyone practises the principle of 'win-win' in their negotiating. Some would rather use poor ethics in trying to 'win' at any cost. Examples of poor ethics include:

- physical discomfort (like having you face a window with the sun shining in your eyes);
- false authorities (telling you that he can make all decisions, when he cannot);
- personal bribes;
- false information;
- false incentives;
- half truths; and
- falsified records.

If you are ever in the position of being subjected to any of these tactics, tell your opponent that you know what he is doing, and that you want it corrected or stopped immediately. If he refuses, you should refuse to go on.

Before beginning any negotiation, make certain that you know what your opponent's power is, as well as your own. What is more important? What are the alternatives? It is advisable to gather as much support as possible for your proposal before presenting it; and if possible try to negotiate on home turf.

Leverage

Leverage – who needs whom the most? Once you know the answer to this, you can gauge your negotiations accordingly. Try to find out from your customer's staff how badly they need you. Time is a key element. Whoever is most constrained by time will make the most concessions at the eleventh hour. You must, however, be aware of your own true deadlines and the severity of the consequences if you go over them.

There are ways you can create deadlines for your prospects. Things like: 'the offer is good until . . .' or 'our price goes up as of . . .' are great at creating some pressure for him to make a decision. Because most concessions are made near the deadlines, save your most important points for then. The one thing you have to avoid is 'dropping a bomb' at the last minute, by making a brand new demand that wasn't previously discussed. This is almost sure to cause all of your work up to that point to collapse. Instead, talk about the issues early on without pressing for an agreement. Remember, as you near an agreement your adversary is far more likely to make concessions because of all the time he has already invested in the negotiations.

When negotiating, it is imperative that you know precisely what it is that you want, and what you may be willing to concede (no matter how reluctantly). As stated earlier, you must also know how badly your prospect needs what you have. One should not be lulled into a sense of false security by believing that he doesn't know your weaknesses. He probably has a better idea than you realize. It is up to you to disguise or minimize your weaknesses with plausible explanations about why they aren't very important.

Please . . . don't ask

What happens when you get put on the spot by one of those lip biting, right-to-the-core type of questions: 'What will you do if I don't sign the contract?' Simple. Rephrase the question so that it becomes one that you are prepared to respond to, and then answer it, giving as much information as possible. You do this so that the original question is not repeated. If your opponent insists, however, you can do one of several things:

- answer a question with a question;
- qualify your answer;
- argue the relevancy of the question;
- tell him that you have to think about it;
- tell him that you have to consult someone; or
- act stupid (this works like a charm).

If you know your opponent's true position, and have all the information about him that you need, you can go ahead and make the first offer. If, however, you are still in doubt about either his true position or his needs, let him do most of the talking. He will either offer something himself, or, while he is talking, you may get the facts that you need in order to proceed.

Any time that you make an initial offer, keep your aspiration level *realistically* high or low (depending upon your position). Once you get into concession-making, never, but never, give something away for nothing. Always ask for a like concession from your customer beforehand. Keep your concessions small and infrequent, and do not make large concessions before he does. If anything, you are best to make your concessions smaller, not larger – especially if it pertains to price.

Patience is a virtue

Probably the most effective means by which you can come out of negotiations with what you want is through patience. Patience can achieve wonders:

1. your account may talk himself out;
2. he may come to understand your position better;
3. the more that your customer talks, the more likely that he will reveal his true position;
4. if you do not appear to be in a hurry, your prospect will probably lower his expectations; and
5. by demonstrating patience, it indicates that you are confident in your original offer.

When your client is making his points, do not interrupt until he has entirely finished. No matter what you may have to say, by cutting him off in mid-sentence, you have cut off any chance of his hearing you. He will still be thinking about what he wants to say, without even listening to anything else. Besides, the one who does most of the talking, gives away most of the information on his position, and hence, makes most of the concessions.

While your customer is talking, take notes and regularly repeat, summarize and verify what has been said. You want to make absolutely certain that points are understood in the same way by both of you. This will avoid a lot of disappointment and anger later.

Dealing with number two

An excellent strategy to use when you get into serious negotiations, is to tell your client that you are not the one with the final approval. This scenario can generally enhance your position because your opponent will feel that if he cannot strike a deal with you, within the scope of your initial offer, he may have to begin again with your superior. This new individual may want to reopen things already agreed upon.

If you, on the other hand, are negotiating with someone who does not have final approval, insist that whoever does be present and negotiate for himself. If this is not possible, send in your own subordinate. When dealing with a number two person, nail down the agreement one piece at a time, and insist that each point get approved by the boss before continuing.

Emotional impasses

While negotiating, never let your emotions take charge. The old adage about cooler heads prevailing, is also an accurate one here. If your opponent has emotional outbursts, calmly ask him to explain specifically what the problem is and deal with it. If he threatens you, assess the full impact of the threat. If it doesn't have serious consequences or repercussions, either ignore it, or let your opponent know that you are not concerned. If it does, however, confront him, and explain that agreements reached by way of threats have little hope of longevity. React to a threat in the same way as you would to any poor ethic. Refuse to go on if the situation isn't stopped or corrected.

When you reach an impasse, try the 'what if' approach, to see what happens when new variables are introduced. If this still does not break the impasse and there is no middle ground left, you must break off the negotiations with a view to always keeping the door open for the future.

Finally, once you have reached a successful conclusion to your negotiations, make your opponent feel that he has done a great job, and that he has attained something of real value. Good negotiators *never* gloat at the end.

PRICE NEGOTIATION

Every time I think of price negotiations, I am reminded of a quotation I saw written on a plaque in a novelty shop: 'The bitterness of poor quality remains long after the sweetness of low price'. Nothing of value is ever sold for the same price as a cheap imitation. If we want quality, we have to be willing to pay for it. This message has to be repeated to your customer time and time again. The strange thing is, she probably believes in this principle when it comes to buying articles for herself, but she wants you to believe that it doesn't apply to business. Once you have destroyed the myth, both you and she can get down to realistic price negotiation.

John Ruskin once said: 'There is hardly anything that man cannot make a little worse and sell a little cheaper – and the people who consider price only, are his legal prey.' And prey they are. Only a fool would believe that all things are made equal, irrespective of cost and therefore price. Basically, people's human nature will drive them to buy a cheaper product if they feel that they will get the same benefit from it. This is a big if. Most times, however, cheap products are built down to a price, rather than up to a standard. It is up to the professional salesperson to make this point not only understood, but acknowledged by his or her accounts.

Justifying your price

Rarely does a customer know the true price of any product that she buys. By offering you less and getting your reaction, she can begin to zero in on what she feels it should actually be. Undoubtedly, everyone wants to get full value for their money and therefore you have to make sure that she understands the difference between what you are offering and her alternative. For example, many times all of her tangible costs are not fully known by the prospect. Things like handling, transportation, insurance, inventory and warehousing have to be considered. Then there are the invisible costs which are no less real: lost sales due to out of stock situations; penalties for late completion of work; idle workers waiting for a part, etc. All of these intangibles have to be considered in order to derive full costs. Any time you speak of price, it must be viewed in connection with:

- quality;
- service advantages;
- company reputation;
- advertising;
- promotional assistance, and
- after sales service.

Here, the expression 'translate features into benefits' should read: 'translate *costs* into benefits'.

Generally, the more product differentiation a firm enjoys, the more independent it can be in setting its prices. There must be, however, a correlation between costs and prices for there is always an alternative, no matter how good your product is. Companies must offer a fair price if they are to be successful. Almost any buyer is willing to pay a fair price, when she knows no one else is getting a better one.

The essential thing that a salesperson has to do when closing a sale, is to justify the price. It must be demonstrated that the product is a quality product and the price is a fair price. It is up to the salesperson to convince the buyer of that. Think about it: if your product were free, you wouldn't have to worry about giving it away, therefore it must have a value. That value should also be the price level already set by the company. Competition ordinarily sees to that. Most salespeople almost expect objections to be raised with the price quotations. Always discuss product – then price.

So, when do you quote your customer your price? I have always left it to the buyer to ask. Why? Well, if the buyer does not bring up the question of price, there is no need for you to do it. The longer you have to explain what it is *exactly* that you are selling, the easier it is for the buyer to realize its value. Perhaps price is not even a major concern. By your raising the issue, the buyer will feel compelled to begin a rigorous examination of your price against your competitor's. Let's face it, not every customer has a fixation about being overcharged. The thing to remember is that although the price will have to be quoted eventually, it can be given when you write up the order. If neither the buyer nor you make a big deal over the price, it can be handled in a very 'matter of fact' manner.

One final reason for never quoting a price to an unsold buyer is because the salesperson needs time to determine what the customer is actually buying. Once this is known, sell those features until the prospect is sold.

Price objections

Price objections fall into one of four categories:

1. the buyer may believe the objection to be true;
2. the buyer may have a lower quote;
3. the buyer uses this as a brush-off; and
4. budget restraints.

Never defend your price directly. Turn the objection into a question to find out more specific information. Frequently, buyers who say that your price is too high, are not clear on its:

1. value;
2. quality;
3. dependability;
4. benefits;
5. advantages exclusive to your product; or
6. advantages exclusive to your company.

None the less, we come to expect the issue to be raised, so be prepared. There are many ways to overcome the objection. Following, are several comebacks that I have found to be effective:

- 'Where is our price too high? Our company is usually very competitive?' Here, get the specifics and deal with them.
- 'How much are we out of line?' If she tells you and you know the competitive product, make direct comparisons. Show the buyer the additional benefits she gets with your product and price.
- 'Are your other quotes based on the exact specifications that ours is?' Frequently they are not.
- 'Your company sells quality. I have seen it in all your advertisements. To sell a quality product you need quality components, and that is what I am offering. I don't believe your

company cuts down on costs when it affects quality, and neither does
mine.'
■ 'We couldn't stay in business if our prices were out of line. Quality
to price, ours is the best on the market and I would like to show you
why.'

There are numerous other comebacks to price objections and you
should always be prepared to use the right one at the right time, on the
right customer. Notwithstanding all the sales finesse in the world, there
are bound to be times when you have to come down on your price to get
the order. Never, positively never, come down either too quickly or too
much. If you do, you may as well close your briefcase and pick another
profession. You will never get sales like that. All you have done is
convince the buyer that you were out to overcharge her in the first place,
even if it is not true. It stands to reason that although you may appear to
be offering her a fantastic deal, she will refuse it because she can't trust
anything you say. Rather than giving big discounts, why not break the
difference down between your price and what she has been offered;
then amortize the difference over the life of the product. A case in point
would be an item that lasts for 12 months and costs £365 more. That may
sound like a big difference but a pound a day might take the sting out of
it.

On the point regarding budgetary constraints, which may be
legitimate, find out who has the authority to override the budget and get
him or her into the meeting. If you can convince this individual of your
product's worth, the budget may not be such a major obstacle after all.
Remember, your price is right . . . sell it.

In closing this chapter on negotiations, I would like to quote another
John Ruskin reference to the low bidder:

> It's unwise to pay too much, but it's worse to pay too little. When you pay
> too much, you lose a little money, that is all. When you pay too little, you
> sometimes lose everything, because the thing you bought was incapable of
> doing the thing it was bought to do. The common law of business balance
> prohibits paying a little and getting a lot, it can't be done. If you deal with
> the lowest bidder, it is well to add something for the risk you run. And if
> you do that, you will have enough to pay for something better to start
> with.

9

Sales and Marketing

It is folly to believe that companies are in business to produce and then sell products. What they are in business for is to make profits – full stop. Making profits today poses some serious problems because of the intensity of the competition that every organization has to deal with. Competition is not only desirable, however, it is indispensable if we are to improve the products that we sell and upgrade the service that we provide.

In essence competition makes us sharper. If you can consistently outperform all others that you sell against it is probably because you are doing something that they are not – solving problems. Sales is one of the few professions where you not only expect to encounter problems, but you actually go out looking for them. Problems are opportunities in disguise.

Most if not all of our best sales opportunities come from a buyer's unfulfilled needs. How can you spot problems or needs that others may miss? What can you do to obtain a competitive edge with your customers? Note the following suggestions:

- Notice details that are ignored by others.
- Rearrange components in the marketing chain to improve the final product or service.
- Try adding something new to the mixture (new packaging for instance).
- Be imaginative; focus on the unusual.

Opportunities abound. All it takes is someone to see them:

> *They do me wrong who say I come no more*
> *When once I knocked and failed to find you in,*
> *For every day I stand outside your door*
> *And bid you wake and rise to fight and win.*
> *But when opportunity does knock by some uncanny quirk*
> *It often goes unrecognized – it so resembles work.*
> (Anonymous)

MARKETING WARFARE

This title sounds ominous, doesn't it? Warfare! Most people tell you it's a jungle out there when in reality it is a battlefield; salespeople are in the trenches. Because it is a battlefield with us in the middle of it, we are faced with two choices: we can either stay where we are and let people take 'pot shots' at us or we can attack! I believe we should attack; take the initiative; be a general.

First, before we attack there are certain things that every good general will want to know.

Position

Where are you in relation to the enemy?
(Decoding: Are you the market leader? If not, are you close enough to try to take him out? Is your company somewhere in the middle of the pack? Are you the new kid on the street?)

Battleground

(Decoding: We would immediately say that the customer's office is the battleground, and this is partially correct. The real battleground however, is in our customer's mind. More on this later.)

Warfare

What kind should be deployed?
(Decoding: Do we go on the offence or take up a defensive position? Should we try to out-flank or use guerrilla tactics? The answer to these questions will depend upon your company's position.)

Strategy

(Decoding: The strategy used must be based on company position and the type of warfare being fought.)

Wait, don't pull these pages out and burn them; at least not yet. We do need marketing warfare and I will prove it to you before this chapter is finished. For a start, don't we launch 'campaigns' in our business? Haven't you 'gathered intelligence' about your competition? What about your latest promotion to win new customers – 'surprise attack'. Or how about the 'strategy' you are using to 'break into' 'target' accounts? Is it a coincidence that much of our sales jargon sounds like something out of the military? No, it isn't. Consciously or unconsciously we practise many of the principles of warfare in our sales work every day. If we are aware that we are doing so, and want to work on that premise, we can get the full benefit of the experience of some of the great military minds that came before us.

Carl von Clausewitz was a Prussian general who was considered as much a philosopher as a soldier. His book, *On War*, which was printed in 1832 is still rated by many as being the best publication ever written about the principles and strategies involved in waging successful warfare. It is from his observations, more than a century and a half ago, that we can succeed on our modern day battlefield – provided we are willing to learn and apply these lessons.

There is every reason to believe that his formula for winning and our own, can be the same. Of all the reasons, however, the most important one is that history repeats itself. This includes the history of past actions and reactions of our competitors. It is because of this that we can plot a solid course into the future. So, let's begin.

1. *The objective*: Know what you want to accomplish.
2. *Offensive action*: Go and do – don't sit and think.
3. *Concentration of forces*: Use strength against your competitor's weakness.
4. *Surprise*: Don't let outsiders know what you are planning.
5. *Flexibility*: Have a fall-back position and a secondary objective.
6. *Simplicity*: Make sure that everyone understands the objective and plan.
7. *Timing*: King Agesilaus of Sparta said it best: 'It is circumstance and proper timing that give an action its character, and make it either good or bad.'

MARKET POSITION

Now that we have established the principles of marketing warfare we are ready to look at market positions.

Market Leader – Defensive

When you are the market leader you must take up a defensive position. After all, the market leader is ahead and wants to keep it that way. To coin an old cliché, *the best defence is a strong offence*. The leader attacks first. They do this through all forms of media. They are continually on their guard against competitive moves so that they can put up an effective block. Clausewitz said: 'The statesman who, seeing war inevitable, hesitates to strike first, is guilty of a crime against his country.'

Contending Market Leaders – Offensive

They usually have the resources to attack the leader head-on. They concentrate their efforts on the leader's weakest point.

Mid-size Companies – Flanking

They usually take over non-contested areas. When they attack, they do so suddenly and unexpectedly, and then follow through with constant pressure.

Small-size Companies – Guerrilla

Only small segments of the market can be defended due to limited resources. If a situation goes badly for them, they abandon it quickly.

Now let's go to the battleground.

MENTAL LIST

As I mentioned earlier, the real battleground lies in the customer's mind. It is there that new information is accepted or rejected. If the new data she receives is consistent with what she already believes, no problem; it gets accepted and entered. If, however, she is told something that goes against what she has always believed to be true, then we can expect a struggle in replacing the old and bringing in the new. This theory, more than anything else, applies to what she believes about certain products or companies. She has a *mental image* in her mind of who, or what, is first on her mental list.

The most common way of becoming number one on her mental list is by being first to bring a product to the market, and by using the greatest efforts to promote it. In other words, to have you and your product become synonymous. There are a few brilliant examples of this: Hoover, Coke, Brillo pads. Aren't these the things we ask for when we want a 'vacuum cleaner', 'cola soft drink' or a 'scouring pad'? In these three cases the brand name became the household name! Also, it should be pointed out that the emphasis is not on who invented the product, but rather who marketed the product first. Pizzas were just pizzas until Pizza Hut took over. Sperry-Rand invented the computer but IBM was the first to market it correctly.

For these reasons, being there first *and in force*, has long-term benefits. It also explains why some market leaders continue to do well even though their products may be lagging behind their competitors'. They enjoy the image and position that the others do not. They are first on the customer's mental list.

It is not always easy to knock out the bloke holding down the number one position. Realistically, in some cases, it may not even be in your best interest to make the attempt. Much depends upon your cash flow and human resources. To take over the top market spot demands a great deal of advertising money to attain the position, and an equal or greater amount to stay there. Another, and perhaps better solution to taking over, may be to invest all this advertising money in research and development. You may be able to come up with your own 'market first' and obtain the number one position by this means.

We can conclude, therefore, that some market positions should not be contested. Going head-to-head with a very superior competitor could leave you with a colossal headache and an empty bank account. It may be preferable to only attack his weak spots, develop your own dominant market positions or go after someone less formidable.

TYPES OF WARFARE

Defensive

In defensive warfare you, as the leader, should pick the battleground and initiate your own actions. Be proactive instead of reactive. Do not imitate your competition or be panicked by their successes. As the leader you must exhibit composure.

Offensive

As the word implies, here we take both the initiative and the action. The most important rule in offensive warfare is that you must have the resources before you begin, and the resolve to follow it through to the end. Clausewitz had a rule for this, '. . . it is very difficult . . . for the most talented general to gain a victory over an enemy double his strength.'

Flanking

In flanking warfare you must develop an identity for your company and your product. Let your customers know what you stand for and what they can expect from you that they can't obtain elsewhere. Clausewitz stated: 'Where an absolute superiority is not attainable, produce a relative one at the decisive point by making skilful use of what you have.'

Guerrilla

Here, some units continually surprise their opponents with *unpredictable* tactics. Mao Tse Tung said:

> The enemy advances, we retreat
> The enemy encamps, we harass
> The enemy retreats, we pursue.

The lesson here is that the little man should take what he can, when he can. Take advantage of opportunities when they come along. The 'big boys' don't do everything well and there are always openings (unfulfilled needs) for those alert enough to see them.

STRATEGIC PLANNING

We now have the basics for our position, the battleground and the different types of warfare that we can wage against our competition. Next, we are ready for our strategy. 'Strategy fixes the point where, the time when and the numerical force with which the battle is to be fought.' Clausewitz adds to his definition, 'there is no more imperative and no simpler law to strategy than to keep the forces concentrated,' and 'all forces which are available and destined for a strategic object, should be simultaneously applied to it.'

In strategic planning timing is critical. For example, if you are in a defensive position you may want to postpone the battle until the timing is better for you. If, on the other hand, you are taking the offensive, you pick the time when the elements are most in your favour and least in favour of your competitor. Once you begin, secrecy and swiftness are essential, as is the focusing of your attack where your adversary is not focusing his attention.

If you are fortunate enough to have a competitor making a lot of bad moves, follow Napoleon's doctrine: 'Never interrupt your enemy when he is in the process of making a mistake.' This principle, no matter what market position you hold or the type of warfare that you are conducting, will win your battles for you.

Now, to put these principles into perspective for the modern day battles, let's take an example of how they can be applied to your everyday sales work.

CASE STUDY

You are working for a mid-sized company manufacturing hardware and tool supplies. The market leader has the market well covered through extensive distribution and advertising/promotion. Your sales are sluggish and you are experiencing difficulty in trying to sell your top-line product against theirs. What to do?

Solution

To begin with, yours is a mid-sized company so you should take up a flanking position. Remember, flanking positions usually involve taking over non-contested areas. Let's face it. The market leader that you compete against is good and he has a complete array of products to sell. But does he concentrate his efforts on selling his entire line or only a few of his major products?

The answer is simple. He will go after and heavily promote his 'big ticket' items where profit margins are greatest. He will trust that his company reputation and market presence will pull his entire line along the road to success. But will it? Yes, if you go head to head with him against his premier products, where he has the edge. (I know you don't believe that he has an edge over you, but in his customer's mind, he does.) If, on the other hand, you concentrate your efforts and attack the products that he isn't pushing, you may be able to develop an identity for yourself and your company. In essence, you can attain a relative superiority for these certain products over his. You can become the winner of this particular battle in the customer's mind.

Let's review the steps leading up to this victory:

1. *Objective*: Your goal is to attain the number one position on the secondary product line.
2. *Action*: Offensive. The battle begins when your competitor least expects it – when he is promoting something else.
3. *Concentration of forces*: Every call you make will have his secondary products as your primary objective.
4. *Surprise*: Keep your plan within company walls. Don't tell your customers what it is that you are trying to accomplish.

5. *Flexibility:* If the customer you are seeing isn't interested in these products, don't push the issue. Your fallback position is to sell him the products that he will buy.

6. *Simplicity:* Do all the key people in your organization know what you are doing? What effect will your actions have on their departments? For instance, marketing, purchasing, traffic, customer service, order processing and/or your warehouse may have to make adjustments to ensure that what you are selling can be delivered. Internal communication is essential to your plan's success.

7. *Timing:* When the market leader is concentrating on something else.

There we have it. There is no big secret to becoming successful in the war you wage every day. All it takes is the willingness to learn from the generals and the determination to put your plan into action.

10
Selling Tools

CUSTOMER TYPES

The first tool to be used in selling is your thorough knowledge of the types of customers that you will be dealing with. You may question whether or not this is a tool, but in reality it is among the most important. In the same way that an architect needs a blueprint to successfully build an office tower, you need to know what kind of people you will be seeing in order to successfully deal with them.

If you wanted to prepare a comprehensive list for every type of personality that you could chance upon, I doubt that this exercise could ever be completed. Every individual is different and how each of us interacts with every other individual is also different. Therefore, in the interests of brevity, we will look at only a few of the basic types of customer characters.

Dodgers

Balkers

These customers are the ones who have extreme difficulty in making up their minds. They generally need a great deal of persuasion. Once you have done your job, sold all the product's benefits and know that this is the right decision for the prospect to make, ask him for the order. When he balks, ask him why he is hesitant. Slowly go over the selling points again. Obtain his agreement on each point before you move on. Get him saying 'yes'. When you have covered all the aspects, and received a 'yes' answer to each, close again. Ask him for the business. He is already in a positive frame of mind because he has been agreeing with you at each step in your presentation. All you are asking for now is one more 'yes'. Frequently at this juncture, you will hear the magic word that you have been working towards. With this type of account, *persistence* is the key.

Nonchalant

Don't you just love these prospects? With her, the best way to get things going, is to 'jump-start' your presentation. Create sudden interest and get her excited. Once you have accomplished this, you have placed her in a frame of mind to buy.

Lookers

We all do this, don't we? How do we get sold when we are only looking? The sales person makes us a special deal (or so we think). Simple but effective.

Lecturers

Talkers

Here we have a group that likes nothing more than talking about anything – except business. If you allowed it, they could spend half an hour talking about the lint in their navel. The only way to get this prospect back on track, is to seize the first opportunity when he may have said anything remotely connected with business. Once this happens, ask him a closed-ended question about his business. Whatever you do, do not be rude or abrupt in effecting this swing-over. Once you have got him back on track, keep him there and sell him.

Egotists

Have you been at a social gathering and heard an egotist? Of course you have. This is the chap, when talking about himself, who looks as if he could talk the ears off a field of corn. Don't you just feel like telling him to 'Shut-up'. Well, you can do that there but not in his office. A much better way is simply to get him to 'hang himself'. They invariably do, you know. The way to set that trap is:

1. Ask his opinions.
2. Give him compliments (not flattery mind you. He may be big-headed but I doubt that he is stupid).
3. Yield on minor issues.

The more he talks about what he wants, what he wants you to do and how he wants to see things happen, the tighter he gets the noose around his neck. Why? Because you are going to follow his advice. If there is a genuine problem, ask him what *he* would do to solve it. There is nothing more gratifying for him than helping lesser mortals.

Know it alls

She wants to impress you, so let her. Give her a chance to talk herself into the sale and she generally will.

Blushers

Clams

This is the 'talkers' opposite number. If you asked her for her lifelong ambition, she would probably say 'to succeed', or something equally profound. The only really successful way of getting this prospect to open up, is to ask open-ended questions. As you continue to probe, she will begin telling you what you need to know. One thing that is common to every individual is that they do want to succeed. You are there trying to help her succeed in doing a better job. Convince her of this through sincerity.

Timid

This next type of prospect needs special handling. Take your presentation slow and easy. Above all else, build the prospect's confidence in you as an individual. When they know that they can trust you and that you are there to help, (without the over-aggressive nature of some salespeople), doors begin to open up. What they are too timid to tell the other bloke, they will tell you because they feel more comfortable about doing business with you rather than with him.

Curious

Here the best tool is to work on the buyer's ego and pride. A little 'show-biz' style may go a long way in gaining her interest and business.

Browbeaters

Sceptics

These are my personal favourites. A good sceptic usually provides you with your first and strongest line of defence against any competitor. The sad fact is that most salespeople don't have convincing enough arguments to persuade this type of prospect and he therefore remains available for the right salesperson. Be prepared to use proof (and lots of it) for virtually everything you say. It is crucial that you obtain his agreement on your points as you go along. Once you have landed this account, notwithstanding the blood, sweat and tears, he is yours, unless you screw up, or someone else comes in with a better argument. Chances are, however, if you were good enough to get him in the first place, he trusts you. Therefore, if he is contemplating a change, he will probably want to check with you on the merits of your products versus the new fellow's. This tip, that the account may be in jeopardy, should not be taken lightly. Get back in there to reinforce his belief in you and your product.

Bullies

These guys are as good an ally for you as the sceptic. Amazingly, his tactics work on the vast majority of salespeople – or else why would he continue to use them? He is the six foot four inch gorilla, who probably gets beat up at home by his five foot two inch wife. When he comes into the office he feels like taking it out on someone – you. You, however, stand your ground and avoid arguing with him. You stick to the basics of probing for his wants and needs.

In a very short time, when he discovers that you are not going to be intimidated, King Kong transforms into the pussy cat he probably is, and you can get down to the business of getting his business. Remember, you are not some masochist flunkey who came by his office to get dumped on. You came because you had something important to talk to him about.

Rude

We all too often come across these types, don't we? Well, let's face it, everyone, including you and I, is in this position from time to time, perhaps without even knowing it. An argument at home, bad news in the office, fatigue or any number of circumstances can put someone in an off mood. The cure for an individual in this mood is empathy. Offer friendship and kindness. The last thing this prospect needs, is a high-pressured, aggressive sell. Get her mind off her troubles. Relax her and make a low-key presentation. Once her hostilities have been calmed, she is in a frame of mind where you can make your sale.

Philosophers

Thinkers

Your best approach here is the soft-sell. Show her you are a thinker too. In this way, you will gain her respect, become closer to her as a person, and then wind up with her business.

Good Natured

Thank goodness for these accounts. Although he is approachable, he is not necessarily an easy sell. Make sure that you have got your facts and figures straight and give him a professional presentation. Charm, rather than high pressure, will win over this prospect.

CUSTOMER GROUP

Next, in looking at the broad outline of what components make up a prospect, we must take into consideration the significance of his group.

Age

Young

The young business professionals are quite often the movers and shakers in their organization. They reached their current positions through hard work and by approaching old problems with new ideas: fresh, innovative, perhaps revolutionary ideas. Your best approach is to build enthusiasm, get them excited and keep them that way. Don't be afraid to use emotion. Illustrate to this prospect that what you have to sell is what she needs to continue her trend of improving her company's position, as well as her own. Do this and you have got the sale.

Middle-Aged

A most important rule in dealing with middle-aged managers, is to show respect. In all likelihood, they have been with their firms a good number of years and feel that they worked hard to be where they are. Build this manager's ego and become someone that can be relied upon.

Elderly

With this prospect, follow the example of the tortoise – be slow and sure. Show respect for his years, experience and position. Demonstrate empathy for his problems. It is imperative that you gain his trust and *apply no pressure*. Be patient. Take as much time as is needed to gain his approval of you, your company and your product. One thing is certain, once you have succeeded in getting his business, you are likely to find him a very loyal customer.

Ethnic Origin

It is extremely difficult to generalize your best customer approach based on ethnic origins. However, let's not kid ourselves; there are certain dos and don'ts that should be followed based on people's customs and beliefs. Through your own contact with people, you will undoubtedly develop your own list. Again, you may find it helpful to check your records to determine if you are having a less than normal success rate with any given group. If you are, it is time to do some research and polish up that part of your act.

11
Body Language and Listening

BODY LANGUAGE

In trying to effectively understand your customer's attitudes, you need to know what he is really thinking. Customers don't always say what they mean, nor mean what they say. There is no better way of knocking down the walls of his inner fortress than by letting his actions speak louder than his words. Body language can provide us with everything we need to know.

According to past studies on communications, our feelings and attitudes are conveyed through:

Words:	7 per cent
Voice tones:	38 per cent
Body language:	55 per cent

The beauty about body language and its importance to salespeople is that it is extremely hard to control and, more to the point, *it doesn't lie*!

Before we examine the expansiveness of this subject, perhaps a few words on the other two forms of communication would be worthwhile. Certainly, the first needs little explanation. Words, after all, are how we *thought* everything got properly communicated. Reading about body language will change this view. The second, voice tone, is also fairly comprehensible. Anger, happiness, scepticism, sorrow, are all immediately recognizable. Other voice tones can add meaning to words. Breathing sounds for example, can also tell us quite a bit:

■ Coughs denote insecurity and uncertainty.
■ Sighs denote wishfulness.
■ Yawns denote boredom or disinterest.
■ Grunts denote general agreement.

When we combine the words with the tones, and then combine these with the body signals, we come as close to the actual truth as we are going to get.

There is both good and bad body language. Good body language produces:

■ good eye contact;
■ firm, erect body posture; and

■ open gestures that move towards the person who is speaking.

All of these gestures show confidence.

Poor body language, however, produces:

■ no eye contact;
■ fidgeting;
■ nervousness; and
■ poor posture.

Left to right movement communicates insecurity or doubt. A controlled position conveys tenseness. Forward and backward motions indicate positive receptiveness.

Eight Ways to Say It

There are so many ways the signals are sent, we are best to categorize each and list the action that transmits the signal.

1. Superiority:
■ fingertips touching;
■ hands on hips;
■ hands behind neck;
■ palm down handshake;
■ piercing eye contact.

These are all meant to intimidate. Do not allow them to do so.

2. Disinterest:
■ shuffling papers;
■ playing with objects on desk;
■ doodling;
■ looking around the room;
■ no eye contact.

Regain the prospect's attention before continuing your presentation.

3. Antagonism:
■ redness of skin;
■ clenched fist;
■ negative shake of head;
■ pursed lips;
■ crossed arms or legs.

It is best here to acknowledge the signal(s) and probe for its cause(s).

4. Nervousness:
■ hand wringing;
■ fidgeting;
■ head down;

■ shifting from side to side;
■ minimum eye contact.

Make every effort to relax the prospect and put her at ease.

5. Indecisiveness:
■ fingers to mouth;
■ biting lip;
■ scratching head;
■ puzzled look;
■ neck pulling.

You are best to slow your presentation or pause in order for the prospect to have time to gather his thoughts. Once you have done this, you can begin probing again. Be sensitive to the prospect's uncertainties.

6. Dishonesty:
■ touching nose while speaking;
■ ear pulling;
■ covering mouth while speaking;
■ crossed arms and legs with body leaning forward;
■ no eye contact;
■ nose gets longer (sorry, I couldn't resist)!

Probe for the cause of your prospect's reaction to something *you have* said.

7. Assessment:
■ chin stroking;
■ index finger to lips;
■ glasses in mouth;
■ raised eyebrows with head tilted back;
■ good eye contact.

Use your own positive signals to show interest in what she is saying and proceed with your presentation.

8. Honesty:
■ leaning forward in seat;
■ back and forth movement of the body;
■ open hands;
■ smiling;
■ good eye contact.

These are the actions and traits that *you* should use in transmitting your own signals. If your client is doing likewise, you can be assured of his receptiveness to what you are saying.

When reviewing the various lists, it is important to look for several signs and not just one gesture to determine what the prospect is really saying.

Body Motion and Position

Your prospect's body angle offers a very important and simple clue to how your presentation is going. If she leans towards you, she is sending a positive signal; away from you is negative. Likewise, this same rule applies to you. Give your client a positive signal by leaning forward during your presentation. Even if the prospect isn't consciously aware of body language, her subconscious is!

As mentioned earlier, back and forth body movements are positive, whereas side to side movements transmit insecurity. Stillness or too much movement project nervousness. Keep alert to these signals and do not fall into bad habits yourself.

Eye contact is extremely important in getting an accurate reading of what your account is thinking. If she is trying to hide what she is thinking, she will avoid direct eye contact as much as possible. On the other hand, increased eye contact signals honesty and interest. Also, watch for pupil dilation. Dilation occurs when there is strong emotion.

The positioning of the arms also provides a good gauge for either positive or negative signals. Arms or forearms on desk towards the speaker are positive signals. A negative signal is, of course, the reverse of this – arms off the desk and away from you.

Open or relaxed hands are very positive. Self touching gestures indicate tension and, tightly clasped hands are very negative.

This may seem strange, but it is true none the less. No sales are made when your prospect has his or her legs or ankles crossed. These signals denote reservation or defensiveness. Before you can hope to make the sale, your customer's feet should be flat on the floor; this simply means that he or she is open and ready for business.

After having said everything about signals and what to watch for, the obvious question is – where can I possibly sit to get such a bird's eye view? It may not always be possible, but try to sit in a seat *beside* your client's desk. In this way, your prospect must turn towards you and you will have an opportunity to see every body movement. Normally when you enter your customer's office, the visitor's chair is directly in front of the desk. What I frequently do to reposition my chair, is quite simple but effective. I ask my client if he or she would mind if I came over to the side of the desk to have a better angle to show items of interest in my literature. Rarely does this approach fail to work.

Never be lulled into too much self-confidence because your presentation got off to a good start. Always be scanning your customer's signals during the meeting. They will act as your barometer in gauging whether to continue, slow down or redirect your approach.

If you begin to sense that your client is sending out mildly negative signals, you are better to deal with them immediately before they turn into fully fledged antagonistic signals. In any case, until the problem is dealt with, little of the message you are trying to convey will be absorbed. Taking care of your customer's problem must come first.

Sensory Signals

Finally, after all the signals have been properly noted and deciphered, you come down to the close. At this point our prospects fall into one of these categories:

Visual Prospect

Says things like, 'It's clear to me', 'Show me', etc. When closing here, include pen and pad demonstrations.

Auditory Prospect

Says things like, 'It sounds right', 'It's got a good ring to it'. When closing, make statements that must be answered affirmatively. Get her saying yes on your point-by-point build-up, and then she will say yes to giving you the order.

Action Prospect

Says things like, 'We'll kick that around', 'It's a shot in the arm'. Be very descriptive in what actions will result from buying your product.

Make sure that in your enthusiasm to get all of these things right, you don't break a cardinal rule: never invade your client's breathing space. There is a distance of two to four feet that is entirely his (that includes putting your briefcase in this area as well). Ensure that you give him the space to be comfortable.

EFFECTIVE LISTENING

It has been said that the beginning of wisdom is silence. The second stage is listening. Common sense will tell you that you will never learn anything if you are doing all the talking. When you want to impress someone, it is tempting at times to spout off at the mouth and talk about how good you are. Big mistake! There is a great quotation in Og Mandino's book, *The Greatest Salesman in the World*, that covers this quite adequately: 'Yet, never will I proclaim my accomplishments. Let the world, instead, approach me with praise and may I have the wisdom to receive it in humility.'

Rather than trying to impress your customer with self-praises, attempt to learn something new from her. Not only does this approach stroke her ego (everyone likes to impart jewels of wisdom to his listener), but what you learn can probably be used to help close a sale.

To listen, really listen, probably begins before either you or she says a word. If you feel and look relaxed you will put your customer in the same frame of mind. No one is going to do much talking if he is tense. The point here is for you to create a setting conducive to easy-going talking, and of course listening.

This whole subject may seem absurd. Surely everyone can listen, right? Wrong! Everyone can hear, not everyone listens. Listening will provide you with everything you will need to know to close a piece of business.

The best place to start listening to your prospect is in your office when you call him on the phone for an appointment. Vibes get sent out over the wires which both you and the prospect respond to. Make a point of smiling when you talk to someone on the phone – in much the same way that you do when you are face to face. This feeling, or 'vibe' gets transmitted, so don't believe that you can call someone up, be distracted, bored or in a lousy mood and that he will be excited about talking to you, or eventually seeing you. Your voice inflection will tell him the truth.

Dos and Don'ts

Here are some dos and don'ts for effective listening:

Do:
- Limit your own talking.
- Keep the customer's point of view in mind.
- Concentrate.
- Prepare in advance.
- Take notes.
- Listen for ideas.
- Listen for overtones.
- Practise.

Don't:

- Think of what you are going to say next.
- Try to talk and listen at the same time.
- Be afraid to ask questions.
- Interrupt.
- Argue mentally with your prospect.
- Jump to conclusions.
- Try to write everything down.
- React to the person; but *do* react to the idea he expresses.

Poor listening, not listening or monopolizing the conversation can have a disastrous effect. If you do not listen, he will not listen. If you do not ask questions, he will not ask questions. If you do not show interest or involvement, your actions will produce a mirror effect.

The truth is that you can't discover your prospect's needs, if you are either doing most of the talking or little of the listening. If your customer senses that he is not engaged in a genuine two-way conversation with you, with equal exchanges, he may just cut the meeting off where it is. You don't have much of a chance of selling anything when you are standing on the wrong side of the door.

Seven Golden Rules

Effective listening requires that only a few basic rules are followed:

1. Look at the person talking. Eye contact is very important.
2. Ask questions, nod agreement. Let the talker know that you are following what she is saying. Ask closed-ended questions to get the facts, and open-ended questions to draw people out.
3. *Do not interrupt.*
4. Do not change the subject. There is no better way of letting her know that you are not interested in what she is saying. (You should not confuse this rule with getting your prospect on a business track if she is talking about her bridge game.)
5. Check your emotions. Do not over-react to anything she says.
6. Be responsive.
7. Do not allow distractions to get in the way of good listening.

Follow these basic rules and practise them. Effective listening is not a very easy or simple thing to do. Once you have mastered it, however, the rewards and wisdom are plentiful.

12

Selling Techniques

'In great attempts, it is glorious even to fail,' anonymous.

OVERVIEW

Theodore Roosevelt, I think, best summed up exactly what could be the salesperson's motto:

> It is not the critic that counts, not the man who points out how the strong man stumbled or when the doer of deeds could have done better. The credit belongs to the man who is actually in the arena; whose face is marred by dust and sweat and blood; who strives valiantly; who errs and comes short again and again; who knows the great enthusiasms, the great devotions and spends himself in a worthy cause; who at the best knows in the end the triumph of high achievement; and, who at the worst, if he fails, at least fails while daring greatly, so that his place shall never be with those cold and timid souls who know neither victory nor defeat.

This to me, is the essence of selling. We have the power to make things happen. We are there in the arena.

As stated in an earlier chapter, salespeople have roughly 60 seconds, the initial 60 seconds, to make their first impression. If we do not succeed personally, it is also very doubtful that our organization will succeed either. There is a great deal at stake here and we cannot afford to miss our chance. Remember, the first thing that you sell to your customer is *you*.

Convince your prospect that you are a problem solver. Offer her creative ways of improving her business by saving money (cost reductions), or making her life easier (step savers). Assist her in seeing trends in your industry as well as her own. Once you have gained her confidence, she is far more likely to completely open up and discuss her needs – therefore your opportunities. The more valuable you can make yourself to your prospect, the more she will call on you for help. A salesperson does both the customer and ultimately him or herself a disservice if he or she is only interested in getting an order. It is incumbent upon you to make sure that what you are selling is what your customer *wants* and *needs*.

Selling is as much an attitude skill as a technique or ability skill. A positive attitude is essential to winning. Before every call, you must picture yourself succeeding in making the sale. Any salesperson who sees a prospect without the expectation of getting his business, will not be disappointed. Again, this psyching yourself up may sound foolish, but ask any successful salesperson if it works. You really have to put yourself in the right frame of mind. Banish all negative thoughts and substitute these with only strong, positive ones. Review any obstacles in your mind, deal with them and eliminate them. Be yourself. Do not try to become someone else's carbon copy. You are an individual and you are unique. This, as I said earlier, is one of your greatest assets. If you try to look, act or talk like somebody you know, you will seem insincere, when what you want to be is genuine.

At times, it may be difficult to get into a positive frame of mind because of the size of the company you will be seeing. You may feel they are just too small to give you much of a 'charge'. This could be a grave error. A good salesperson should not prejudge a prospect. Situations are not always what they appear to be. This is another exciting facet of what we do. Regardless of the size of the potential order, a professional believes that if a call is worth making, it is deserving of his or her best effort. Never underestimate your customer and end up by selling yourself short.

How much time does a sales call require? This is a fairly easy question to answer. *A sales call should take no longer than the time it requires to get the order!* This could be five minutes or several meetings. The point is, persevere but do not overstay your welcome. Over-talking is often the reason for under-selling. Once in the process of making a sale, neither over-sell nor under-sell. Both result in zero business. Promise what you can do and deliver, but no more. If you reach a point in your discussions where more information or consultation is called for, schedule your next meeting and then leave.

Three qualifications are required to achieve results from a sales call. You need:

1.   obtainable business;
2.   the decision maker; and
3.   the power of persuasion.

Assuming that the first justification has already been determined at the time of making the appointment, we will move on to numbers two and three for discussion.

THE DECISION MAKER

Half the sales battle is in seeing the right person, the one who is authorized to make the purchase – the *decision maker*. No decision maker, no sale. If you are talking to a subordinate, no matter how impressive your presentation is, he cannot buy because he lacks the authority to do so. It is as simple as that. If you are not sure that you are talking to the decision maker, ask the individual you are talking to. This may seem like a delicate issue to raise, but it *has* to be done. There are, however, tactful ways of posing the question, without risking an irreparable insult to the person you may have to see after the sale has been made. You can ask, 'Do you select the supplier, or is that responsibility delegated to someone else in your organization?' By phrasing the question in this way, you won't offend anybody. If the individual you are seeing cannot make the buying decision, you have given him a graceful way out. Similarly, if this prospect is the one who says 'yea' or 'nay', he will probably feel flattered, because you have built his self-esteem by giving him the opportunity to acknowledge his own importance.

When you are certain that you are talking to the decision maker find out exactly what he is buying. This is better known as his '*hot spot*', (remember the story of the two inch drill?). Through good information gathering, and effective questioning, the hot spot will eventually surface. Do not be surprised however, if you get a few 'no' replies when you are trying to close the business. Very often this results from the fact that you have not yet discovered what it is that he is really buying. In fact, unless you are divinely gifted and have your customers buy first time, every time, his first refusal is exactly what you are looking for. In essence, selling does not begin until you get your first 'no'. Many buyers are afraid to buy and so camouflage their real needs in order to brush you off. If you have given a good, thorough presentation, and have answered his questions, his refusal to give you the business means that he is holding back on the real reason he won't buy. He is trying to get rid of you by throwing an objection in the way. Continue to overcome each and every subsequent objection, and eventually his refusals must lead you to his hot spot. Once you know what that hot spot is, that is when you sell. Concentrate all your efforts on that one feature until he can no longer refuse.

PERSUASION AND AIDA

We can persuade a prospect to buy by filling his needs. Before we can fill his needs, though, we have to know what they are. Before we can find out what they are, we must get his Attention, Interest, Desire and Action. We can best remember these four steps through the Italian opera, *Aida*.

To begin with, there are several ways to get a prospect's *attention*:

1. Help the prospect to relax. You can do this through some preliminary small talk, etc. Limit the chit-chat to a maximum of five minutes. By this time her mind is off her problems or other thoughts, and she is in a relaxed and receptive frame of mind.
2. In this five-minute period, talk about her interests. Remember her office is like her trophy room.
3. Try to pay her a *sincere* compliment.
4. Ask her a question on her expertise.
5. Refer to third parties you both know.
6. If you have seen this prospect before, refer to something from your previous conversation: 'How was your holiday?'

After you have succeeded in getting her attention, build her *interest* in one of the following ways:

1. Make the prospect believe there is a benefit she will enjoy.
2. Tell her about something you can do for her.
3. Satisfy her needs. These can be organizational, personal or product related.

Her *desire* comes by way of your presentation, where you prove what you said to gain her initial interest. Always translate features into buyer benefits. Once these three steps are done, you can, and generally will, receive the desired *action*, provided you ask one more question.

ASK FOR THE BUSINESS

As hard as it is to believe, the vast majority of salespeople do not ask for the business. In a study conducted by Business Horizons, over 90 per cent of the salespeople did not ask for a commitment. An astonishing fact, is it not? It is difficult to fathom how someone can do 99 per cent of the selling job and then most often, consciously, neglect to ask for that which they have been working towards. That is like going to university for four years, writing the final examination papers, and then leaving the campus without the results. This raises the obvious question. Why would anybody go through all that effort and then be afraid of asking a simple and deserving question? The answer is *fear of rejection*. It is not surprising that people do not want to be rejected. In sales however, it happens all the time. In fact, if you as a salesperson could close even 25 per cent of the business calls you make every day, you would gather a crowd waiting to see your next feat when you walk on water.

There is nothing wrong with rejection. There can be something wrong, though, with how people handle it. A professional salesperson lives with it daily, grows from it and improves. Some, miscast in a sales role, will crumble under its weight.

It has been said, and I might add, quite accurately, that if even a mediocre salesperson did two things – saw the decision maker and asked for the business – their success rate would astound them.

I once did some work for the president of a large company who was about as subtle as a horse breaking wind. This man gave directness a whole new dimension. He would say something like, 'Can you make a decision or should I talk to your boss?' Not really endearing stuff but I will guarantee you that between his asking this question and eventually the one for the business, he was more effective than 90 per cent of the people out there pounding the pavements today. Rather than giving up, learn to overcome this problem and be successful.

13

The Presentation

Here is where we really find ourselves in the trenches. The moment of truth, the reckoning: the presentation. The simple law of selling will tell you that if you can't open, you can't close. Every presentation should be designed with the overview that no one likes to be sold, but everyone likes to buy. During the course of your presentation, give your prospect the reasons to buy and then guide her smoothly to that final decision. Every prospect buys from somebody – let it be you.

In any communication, direct or indirect, the message should meet three criteria:

1. It must be designed and delivered in such a way as to get the prospect's attention.
2. Words, expressions or signals, must be understood by the buyer and seller in the same way.
3. It must highlight buyer needs or desires and indicate the way in which they can be met.

If one had to draw up a report card on the essentials involved in a sales presentation, it might look something like this:

Manner	(20 per cent):	it should be easy, sincere, and not nervous.
Voice	(20 per cent):	it should be clear, firm and alive.
Words	(10 per cent):	good vocabulary and grammar.
Delivery	(10 per cent):	neither too hesitant nor too fast.
Subject	(20 per cent):	comprehensive knowledge and coverage.
Closing	(20 per cent):	timing and asking for the business.

SELECTING THE RIGHT APPROACH

There are several approaches you can take in your presentation.

The *introductory approach* is not generally very effective because it implies too much unfamiliarity; too much getting to know each other is required.

The *customer oriented* proposal is good, provided you already know exactly what his needs are.

The *question* avenue can be filled with perils if unwisely used. The meeting may take on the appearance of an inquisition if it becomes one question after another. The prospect, after all, does assume that you have some knowledge of his business and needs. You should try to space out your questions by dealing with the answer you receive to each, before asking another.

Proven performance advances can be good, provided you have the proof to back up your statements.

Finally, the *customer benefit* appeal is always the best approach. This is what gets the buyer's interest immediately. Tell him what is in it for him.

As you are walking into his office, remember to look around. Let the prospect invite you to sit down. He may just get up and come around his desk to greet you. This is a big psychological plus. It is like the first barrier coming down because he has left his fortress and approached you. Before you get into the facts and figures in your presentation, your prospect is of course relaxed – right? If you sense that he isn't, or, even worse, that he seems to be intimidated by you, try to do something to let him feel that he has the upper hand. Drop something from your case, be a little clumsy. Anything that allows him to *perceive* his control of the meeting is ultimately to your benefit.

CUSTOMER RELATING

Getting through to people is not always easy. There are, however, some ways that you can do this quite effectively just by following some straightforward guidelines:

1. Remember people's names and use them. There is no sweeter sound than hearing one's own name, provided it is pronounced correctly.
2. Encourage people to talk. If you want someone to talk about herself, try talking about yourself first. If you confide in this individual you can get much closer to her as a person.
3. Talk on her level. Talking like a trial lawyer is fine in a courtroom but not very appropriate in this lady's office.
4. Talk about her interests. Try to find some common ground between you.
5. Compliment her if it is genuine. Insincerity is quickly spotted.

6. Think before you speak. Or, said another way: think twice then speak once.
7. Never argue. You can win the argument and lose the customer. Try to change the subject instead.
8. Be positive and optimistic. This can really rub off on your prospect.
9. Be yourself. Be genuine. If you are out of your normal geographic area for example, do not be afraid to say so. Your prospect will frequently try to put *you* at ease. Also, touching gives the effect of sincerity and empathy. Caution – do not overdo it. You could end up with a face resembling a pizza.
10. Maintain eye contact.

In any sales presentation, it is advisable to keep it clear, crisp and to the point; not stiff or regimented, but to the point none the less. If the buyer wants to talk, oblige him. Just bear your objective in mind. Keep the presentation moving without dragging. If your normal delivery does not seem to be working, start improvising and come up with something more original for this prospect. The guiding principle for a good sales presentation is KISS (Keep It Simple Stupid); it is something we should all practise to perfection. We don't need anything fancy, simply something effective.

Peculiar or interesting business stories are useful. Try to set you, your product and your company apart from the rest of the field. In this way, you will be remembered. Being remembered frequently translates into more sales.

Part of your job in selling the prospect is in helping her to see and recognize what it is that she needs. Believe it or not, the buyer often isn't really clear on this. For this reason, she may not give you many precious hints to help you in discovering how to sell her. This may look bleak, but on the other hand it presents a glorious opportunity. By listening to what she says and picking up on what clues you do get, you can explain your product's benefits. Do not ever assume that she knows what they are because she probably doesn't. Explain them slowly and one at a time to build perceived value. You may just end up hearing her say that your product is exactly what she is looking for.

As part of the persuasion technique, you can definitely appeal to her vanity or ego. Plant seeds in your customer's mind early on in your presentation, and then bring them back later, as if they were her original ideas. If you can succeed in doing this, you can most likely succeed in closing on them. An ego is something that you can work with and generally get predictable results.

GROUP PRESENTATION

If you are making your presentation to a group, do not neglect anyone. If you do, it may come back to haunt you later. That neglected person may actually be the decision maker in the coterie.

There are a number of ways to determine who is leading the pack. It is *not* always the most vocal (look at Japanese customs), nor the most dominant-looking individual there. Be careful. Watch to see where most eyes turn during the conversation. The leader is generally the most interested and asks the most questions but again, there is no guarantee. If, after the first five minutes or so, you still haven't pinpointed the gaffer, start directing all questions to your primary suspect. If he is not the chief, he will eventually turn to the decision maker seeking approval, or guidance in what he is saying.

PLANNING

Irrespective of who you will be talking to, an individual or a group, you must always plan your presentation before sitting down in front of the buyer. You already know that the adoption process for any product or service involves:

- awareness;
- interest;
- evaluation;
- trial;
- decision; and
- confirmation.

Your presentation should be styled to cover each of your points in their respective sequence. You must have a specific objective for making the call. I have seen salespeople 'just pop in' to discuss the profoundness of absolutely nothing and leave with an order book that corresponded exactly with their purpose for being there! Make sure you know why *you* are there.

If you are truly interested in your customer's needs and genuinely try to help her, you will reap substantial rewards. Be on the lookout for a need waiting to be filled. The prospect may not even recognize it at the time, but once you have brought a real need to the forefront, you are helping her do her job. Most people appreciate this kind of help from an expert. When you are laying out your presentation the night before, remember to put yourself in her shoes. What you are offering may make good business sense for you, but will it for her?

QUESTIONING

When discussing customer needs, ask open-ended questions so that you can gain the most information possible. Let the customer do as much talking about his business as he wishes to. If he comments favourably about your service or product, reinforce it by agreeing with his statement, restating the point and telling him about the related benefit(s) associated with his comment.

You should take notes during your meeting, emphasizing to your customer that some of the details should not be trusted to memory (yours not his). Do not overdo the note-taking either. You wouldn't want him to get the impression that you are a court stenographer. You can expand on your own notes when you get out to your car, and add as much detail (including impressions) as you like.

Once into your presentation, avoid closed-ended or leading questions. The former is good to recap his agreement on benefits just before you close. The latter may get you the answers you want, regardless of whether they are right or wrong!

I have always found that a very successful opening question is, 'What criteria do you use in selecting a supplier?' If you listen well, you may just find out what this customer is actually buying. During your meeting, take regular checks on your customer's 'temperature'. Is he warming up to your proposal? Ask him. Say something like, 'how does it sound so far?' If he says that it sounds like a load of BS, then you know you are in trouble. On the other hand, he will probably tell you, 'so far, so good'. By checking on his reaction, it gives you another chance to get more vibes from him before you proceed, or it tells you to back up so you can clear up a point, he either didn't understand, or didn't like. If you hit a lull in the conversation, ask another open-ended question while you regroup.

Ask questions that relate to what your prospect is saying. By doing so, you show him that you are interested and that you are paying attention. If you do not understand something he said, do not be afraid to ask him to explain. First of all, it shows interest. Second, it indicates your sincerity in trying to understand him. Third, that point may be critical to closing the sale. If he asks you a question that you do not have the answer to, admit it. As soon as you can, find out the answer and get back to him.

What happens when you run into a guy who just doesn't want to give you a straight answer? No, don't threaten to make him a eunuch. Get your answers in other ways. Use the roundabout approach. Make statements about the facts that you assume to be correct (however unlikely) and then wait for his response. For example, say something like 'Is the reason you won't buy my product because you are receiving a 25 per cent discount from my competition?' or 'Is my competition offering you special rebates?' He may tell you an obvious lie or, conversely, he may just correct you with honest-to-goodness straight facts. Either way, you are zeroing in on the truth and can concentrate on that for the remainder of your presentation.

Reflective questioning is another excellent way of coming to understand your buyer's opinions or values. For example, if she says: 'Our production rate on widgets is pretty good,' ask her immediately, 'pretty good?' and listen to what she says. She will be obliged to elaborate and you will gain valuable information about her, or her company, in the process.

MR HOSTILE

Difficult customers are not uncommon. Rather than avoiding them, you are best to learn how to cope with their manner and secure their business. There is a lot of business you can do with these people because many salespeople do avoid them. What to do?

1. Don't take what he says personally.
2. Don't try to understand his hostility. Just cope with it.
3. Don't copy his behaviour. Remain quiet, firm and detached.
4. Don't criticize the individual. You may disagree with his ideas but avoid making it a personal attack.
5. Don't expect him to like you. He probably kicks his dog too. Content yourself with the fact that he has agreed to listen to you in the first place.
6. Praise him on his ideas, if you are sincere.
7. Change his stream of abuse into a normal conversation through questioning.

A customer's negative thoughts or views should never be reinforced. Do not lose your cool if the customer insults you, your company or your product. Follow rules one through seven and be professional, even if he isn't.

MISS BICKER

You should not mistake rude customers for those who voice a complaint. We all do this occasionally and we want to be heard. If a customer complains:

1. show sympathy;
2. get *her* facts;
3. get *your* facts;
4. confirm when you will give her an answer;
5. keep your commitment;
6. don't lie;
7. re-sell this account as soon as possible; and
8. never readily admit wrongdoing or error, but show empathy.

A phrase that conveys empathy is: 'I understand how you feel'. Don't say 'I *know* how you feel'; you may get a terrific backlash. By saying you understand, you acknowledge the facts and *sense* how she must feel. You may also say, 'Others felt that way until having considered the following facts.' That makes her feel like she is not alone in her plight. Anyone is entitled to misunderstand something which was not properly explained in the first place. What you do not want to do is to corner your prospect so that she has no graceful or face-saving way out. She won't forget you if you do; and this is definitely not the way that you want to be remembered.

MR RIGID

When you come across strong resistance from a buyer, use diversionary tactics. Get off the subject of your business and onto his. See if you can help him with one of his problems that may not even be related to your products. Change the subject to one that is more interesting to your customer. Ask him about his company's successes or special techniques they use. The point is, look for a small opening anywhere you can find it, to get him back in a more receptive mood.

MRS SATISFIED

What do we do with Mrs Satisfied? We all know her. She is the one who has no need, no inclination to listen to new ideas, no problems, no ambition, no brains . . . But, she does. Ask her closed-ended questions to try to uncover some needs that she may not even be aware of. Use your knowledge of your competitors and what they sell. Single out their weaknesses, and direct your questioning into areas that may be lacking in total customer satisfaction. Be careful when talking to your prospect about your competition. Do not underestimate either of them. If you 'bad mouth' your competition, you imply that anyone using them must be an idiot. The idiot (er, customer) you are talking to probably won't be very grateful for your critique of her business acumen. I have never seen anybody gain anything by talking badly about their competition. If you must say something, say that they are a fine organization with good products. Better still, don't even bring their name into the conversation unless you are unable to avoid it. Do not insult them, and therefore your prospect. Stick to strict comparisons of where you have them beat. Just be prepared to give proof to back up anything you say. Things like sales visuals, testimonials, statistics, trials and analogies can supply the evidence. In reserve, you still have two powerfully convincing weapons – logical arguments and yourself. Use all the firepower that you can muster. Spare nothing that is true and ethical. This is what selling is all about.

Before closing this section on the presentation, there are just two points that should be repeated:

1. Remember that price is the last thing that you should discuss in a sales presentation. What the prospect would have considered exorbitant in the beginning, may now look like a bargain.
2. The buyer may give you a buying signal before, in the beginning, during or at the end of your presentation. When you get the signal, stop talking and close the sale.

14

Overcoming Objections

As was said earlier, selling does not begin until you get your first objection. This is where the 'rubber meets the road'. A word of warning: come prepared. You should never be surprised by any objection a buyer throws at you. If you know your product well, and how your competition operates, you can short circuit the train coming at you, before it derails you. Anticipate obvious objections and inject the answer to them in your presentation.

When handling objections, you must:

1. anticipate them;
2. record them;
3. answer them;
4. disprove or admit to them (then carry on);
5. determine the real objection;
6. disagree in non-argumentative ways;
7. enlist the help of a third party, if required; and
8. try to solve valid objections in some other way.

You may find it helpful to compile a list of fairly standard objections that you come across in your business; then develop a strategy for each. Once you have done this, review your list with your colleagues. See how they overcome them. Then, study and try to improve your strategies on an ongoing basis.

TYPES OF OBJECTIONS

When a buyer voices an objection, it may represent one of several situations: he may believe it; he has possibly heard it; or, as is frequently the case, he is trying to brush you off.

There are six basic types of objections:

1. trivial;
2. false;
3. hypothetical;
4. fearful;
5. absurd; and
6. real.

When you hear the objection, make certain that you have correctly understood it. Either repeat or rephrase it. If it is *trivial*, ask the prospect how important this is to him or his company. If he is honest, he will more than likely tell you it is not very significant and drop it. When it is a *false* objection, it is only a simple matter of supplying the truth, giving him proof that the objection is unfounded. Do not hesitate to call your office from your client's, to confirm any number of facts. He may refuse to buy for a *hypothetical* reason: 'If your service department had a vehicle breakdown I wouldn't get the parts I need, and I would have to shut down my line for the day.' Remember anything that applies to you hypothetically, also applies to your competition hypothetically.

As sometimes happens, the buyer may be *afraid* of making changes in case something goes wrong. This is not a reason to avoid buying. Cushion his fears and offer reassurance. Let him know that he still has the option of going back to his other vendor any time he wishes. *Absurd* objections should never be taken seriously. Although every objection must be acknowledged and dealt with, when a prospect says something totally asinine to you, give him an incredulous look. This should create enough embarrassment for him to stop the charade and drop that line of unreasoning. Finally, we come to genuine objections.

REAL OBJECTIONS

The management of *real* objections requires that the following be done:

1. *Cushion*: Agree with the prospect on the objection but not on the facts.
2. *Real meaning*: Find out what causes her to feel this way.
3. *Respond*: Seldom will words be enough – supply evidence.
4. *Seek Agreement*: Make sure she feels that you have resolved the problem. If not, try again using a different approach.
5. *Close*: Ask her for the business.

No matter how many objections you overcome, ask the buyer for the business once you have dealt with each one. In this way, she will either agree to work with you or, if all of her previous reasons were not the true reasons, you will eventually back her into a corner where she *must* tell you the basis for her refusal.

IRREFUTABLE OBJECTIONS

Occasionally, your prospect will give you an irrefutable objection. Do not try to deny it – admit it. Repeat your strongest benefit. Make it as attractive as possible to the customer's personal desires or needs. If this benefit is also an exclusive one to your product, it may outweigh the benefit you cannot supply. This is the time to try the 'weighing' close.

Use a sheet of paper and write down the 'pros' on one side, and the 'cons' on the other. Or, use your left hand and repeat the benefit or two that you cannot offer, while raising your hand (palm up) an inch or two, after stating each negative point. Then repeat this process using your right hand to indicate the positive points. Once you have done this, you have demonstrated visually, that there are more pros than cons with your product versus the other, because your right hand will be higher than your left. Your buyer now has a mental image of all the things that your product *can* do for her.

EXCLUSIVE BUYING

Another type of objection that you may come across, deals with the prospect who only buys from his personal friends. Loyalty is a great and admirable thing and don't be afraid to let him know that you believe this. However in business, an employee's first loyalty lies with his company. They are the ones who pay his salary, and they are the ones who should get the benefit of the best deal in the marketplace.

When you encounter this problem, check:

1. How long has this exclusive buying been going on?
2. What may the buyer be losing out on?
3. Is your prospect's competitor benefiting by your cost savings?
4. What has his friend done lately?
5. What kind of service is he getting?
6. Does one of your executives know one of his?
7. Does your company have something exclusive to offer?
8. Can this company, or division, be sold indirectly?
9. Who is the back-up supplier for this prospect?
10. Can you break in as a friend yourself?

PROCRASTINATION

Procrastination in purchasing is an excuse that you should rarely accept. When the prospect tells you that she, 'has to think about it', what she is really telling you is that she isn't sold yet. This is as much of an objection, or more correctly phrased 'brush off', as any other. Ask her a series of questions about the product and possible reasons why she doesn't like it. 'Is it the colour? Is it the price? Is it our delivery schedule?' You will end up getting a lot of 'no' answers to these questions, but finally you will hear a 'yes' to the real objection. You can then deal with it and re-sell the prospect. If, however, after asking all these questions, you continue to hear that none of these things is the problem, ask her, 'then what is the problem?' Frequently she will tell you and then you can resume your selling. Caution should be used here. She may simply restate her first position about wanting to think about it. If this happens after you have done your series of short questions, don't push her any further. Accept that she really does want to think about it and ask her when you can see her again to have a decision.

DISINTEREST

If the prospect says that he is not interested in what you are selling, say something like: 'You mean you're not interested in . . .?' Repeat the major advantages of your product or service. Or, 'perhaps you're not interested because you are not aware of . . .' (repeat your major benefit, or cost savings), 'similar companies (name a competitor of his) have been using this product and have indicated to us that they have seen an increase in business.' This should worry the buyer because his competition's increase in business may be at his company's expense. Try to develop some quick attention grabbing phrases like these, and some disinterested accounts may suddenly become very interested.

THE ULTIMATE 'NO'

From time to time, you are going to get a flat 'no' to your request for business. When this happens, don't blame yourself. Ask the prospect:

1. Has she ever had a bad experience with your company?
2. Is there something fundamentally wrong with your product?
3. Was it something you said?
4. Did you miss a point, or not explain something well?

It is worthwhile to find out why she won't buy. She will be doing you a big favour by telling you, because you can learn and improve from it. Also, remember that when a buyer says no she doesn't necessarily mean 'never'. She may simply mean 'not now'. Keep the door open and try again at some point in the future when things may have changed, or your prospects look better. You won't be in the 'penalty box' forever.

15
Closing

A sales person should always keep the close in mind, starting from the moment an appointment is made with the prospect. Concentrating on the close will help with the opening, the qualifying, the demonstration, the presentation and the negotiating. The close completes the selling job.

A quick checklist of the jobs to be done in selling is:

1. Relax the account.
2. Gather information.
3. Determine the decision maker.
4. Determine the hot spot.
5. Sell the hot spot.
6. Overcome objections and ask for agreement.
7. Ask for the business.

If you have done a thorough job with your presentation, answered his unspoken questions and overcome standard objections, the close becomes almost automatic. When closing, ensure that you summarize the benefits that your customer has already agreed upon, and get him saying 'yes', point by point; then ask for the business.

A close is a request for a buying decision: yes or no. A major point to keep in mind, is that most people have difficulty in refusing a direct request. This is why it is so important to ask the question.

BUYING SIGNALS

Closing involves timing. You can get an 'it looks good' buying signal at any time, so be alert for it. Once you receive a buying signal, stop your presentation where it is, concentrate on the signal you have received, and close. For instance, if you are halfway through your discussions and your prospect says, 'what is your minimum order size?' stop what you are doing and ask her what size of order she *wants to place*. If she says, 'can I split the colours 50/50 for an order of 1000?' ask her which two colours you should *send* her. Once she answers your question, write up the order. Any question or sign that you may receive from your account which implies that she is sold, generally means that *she is sold*.

If you have concluded your presentation, handled objections and still have not received a buying signal, don't worry. The timing is still right. You have done your job, so ask for the order. When you have truly handled her hot spot, there really isn't anything else she can do but agree to give you her business.

CLOSING SEQUENCE

When closing a piece of business:

1. Ensure that your prospect is still relaxed.
2. Rebuild his enthusiasm by recapping benefits.
3. Use your customer's words as your ammunition (as a last resort embarrass him, if need be, by reminding him of what *he* said eg 'I would give you this order if you could offer me faster deliveries').
4. Do not use negative words or phrases which may create anxiety for your prospect. Use 'if' instead of 'when'; use 'try' instead of 'buy'; use 'approval' instead of 'signature'.
5. Remain in control, even if he insults you, or buys beyond your wildest dreams.
6. Do not appear to be too excited. He may wonder if he is the only buyer that you have ever had.
7. Don't get brushed off. If he asks an obvious question, ask him what he thinks the obvious answer is.
8. Don't take 'no' for a final answer. Find his hot spot and re-sell him.
9. Make it easy for the prospect to sign the order; have everything ready for his approval in advance.
10. Reassure the buyer that he is making the right decision. 'I won't let you down', 'you can count on me' statements are excellent.

Aristotle claimed that the real show of power is in restraint. As salespeople we naturally like to talk, but we have to know when to restrain ourselves if we are going to close business and keep it closed. Why the question of keeping business closed? Because it is a common fact that most people know how to say nothing, but few know when. It happens virtually every day; salespeople close a piece of business and then *by talking too much*, they end up saying something that collapses all of their hard work and destroys the sale.

Once you have a deal, stop talking about the product altogether. Even while filling out the order form, keep the conversation light and casual. When completed, thank your buyer, shake hands and then get out. Don't talk yourself out of the order. Also, shaking hands is important here because it signifies that the deal is completed and committed to.

THE PERFECT 10

There are many types of closes and it is up to you to decide which one best suits the condition of the call and the prospect. Rather than getting into some 'cute' or 'manhandling' closes, I have elected to give you the basic ways to close business without the 'Hollywood' effect. Some of the other closing techniques that are being used in the marketplace may get results, but I question the ethics involved in frightening people or playing people off against each other. As far as I am concerned, using intimidating closes on your prospect is like sport fishing with depth charges. You may land the fish, but you haven't played by acceptable rules. Winning is important, however the end *does not* justify the means (unless you want 'one time' customers).

Take It For Granted Close

You have answered all the questions and have obtained your customer's agreement on all of your points regarding product benefits. At this stage, simply take out your order book and ask something like: 'When do you want delivery?' or 'How many colour reds should I send?' His direct answer confirms the order.

Either/Or Close

This is where you ask the customer, 'would you rather take delivery now, or wait until your foreman gets back next week?' or 'Would you rather have those in red or blue?' You have not backed her into a corner, have you? You have given her several options!

The Weighing Close

We discussed this in the last section. Just remember, accentuate the positive and play down the negative.

The Trial-Order Close

If the buyer is still extremely nervous about making wholesale changes, just ask her for a trial order to 'see how she likes it'. This normally takes away much of her anxiety. When her trial order works well, get back in there to secure a commitment for all of her business.

It Doesn't Matter Close

When you come across a buyer who enjoys nothing more than giving you a hard time, try closing on his ego. For example, let him know in a discreet way, that you don't really need his business; you are quite successful without it. Let him believe that your product isn't right for everyone. Some people may not be able to afford it, or may not have the training to use it properly. Any of these types of insinuation will quite often spark his interest. He may just buy to prove to you that what you imply, doesn't apply to him.

No Sale Today Close

So, you know that she is not going to buy from you after all. Tell her that you realize this, but would ask a small favour before leaving. Ask her to help you by pointing out where you went wrong. This appeal may very well elicit a reply from her that will tell you what her 'hot spot' is. Now that you have the information, go ahead and start selling your prospect all over again.

What If Close

This is an excellent way of closing the sale almost before you have opened! Make a statement like: 'If I could prove to you that (your major benefit or cost saving), would you buy it?' If what you have said offers a major improvement for the buyer, he will say 'yes'. Just make sure that you can fully prove your claim. Once you have done this, write up the order based on his initial agreement.

What Does It Take? Close

When everything else fails, try this one. Just ask her what you would have to do to get her business. This is not a totally irrational question. Don't expect her to give you a straight answer; in fact she is quite likely to give you something totally absurd. What she may just tell you, however, in a roundabout way, is what you haven't yet sold her on – her real objection.

Classic Close

This is the close to use when you have done all the selling jobs. It is also the one that many salespeople have the most difficulty with. Here, you simply ask a closed-ended question and wait for the answer. What you say is, 'can I have your business?' then *shut up*. The pregnant pause is critical to the total effect that the question has on the buyer's nerves. This may seem like pure nonsense but, whoever talks first in this situation loses. It may take 10–30–60 seconds for his answer, but you *must* wait for it. The psychological pressure will virtually compel him to say 'yes'. Alternatively, if you speak first, you have broken the intensity of the mood, and you have given him a chance to get off the 'hot seat'. Don't let him off easy. If you have done everything well, made a solid presentation and obtained his agreement, you should *expect* to get the order. Don't blow it at this stage. Keep your mouth closed and the order book open.

Dangerous Liaisons

When you appear to have exhausted all avenues on closing a piece of business, there are still a few options open to you. These options are filled with peril, and I certainly don't recommend their use unless there are especially exceptional circumstances. You have to judge for yourself. They are as follows:

1. Go over the buyer's head. This method may work, but needless to say, you have burned a bridge (or better phrased, you have dropped a nuclear bomb on it). If you feel strongly enough about your proposal or suspect foul play on your buyer's part, why not have one of your company executives see one of his? If the sale goes through in this manner, you may still be able to salvage a relationship with a buyer that you will be obligated to see afterwards.
2. See the department head who gave the order to her purchasing department. You may be able to have her specify your product on her purchase order. Again, beware. If this plan works, you will have one individual who isn't really enamoured with your techniques; if it fails, you will have two!
3. See your buyer's buyer. If you have a relationship with your buyer's customer, you may be able to get them to ask for your components when purchasing from your reluctant prospect. You can generally get away with this, provided it is reasonably done in the normal course of your doing business with this third party.

Generally, however, the best course of action to take after a final rejection is to simply thank your prospect for his time and keep the door open. Circumstances, as well as people, change.

REASONS FOR SUCCESS

It is as important to know why you have made a sale as it is to know why you did not. There are many reasons why a sale is made:

- You had a decision maker.
- You sold the hot spot.
- You made a good presentation.
- You have a good product.
- You sold yourself as well as your company.
- You provided facts.
- You followed your plan.
- You showed desire and enthusiasm.
- You were not intimidated.
- You did not argue.
- You did not knock the competition.
- You closed at the right time.
- You asked for the business.
- You left after the sale.

DEBRIEFING

When leaving a sales call, ask yourself these debriefing questions:

1. Did I have a valid purpose for this call?
2. Was the atmosphere conducive to selling?
3. Was I mentally ready to make the call?
4. Was I selling for myself or for the customer?
5. Did I communicate?
6. Were questions asked and answered correctly?
7. Were my responses good and did I listen?
8. Did I handle objections satisfactorily?
9. Did I back up my words with evidence?
10. Did I obtain any real commitment?
11. Did I meet my objective? If yes, why? If no, why not?
12. What should I use or avoid on future calls?

The importance of analysing your work should be quite obvious.

It provides you with the basis to improve for your next call: tomorrow, next week, or next year. We should never acquire skills and then assume that they will always be there. This assumption leads to atrophy. Such is the reality of professionalism: such is the reality of selling. Honesty and hard work avoid the need for making excuses!

16
Conclusions

People have a tendency to be watchers rather than doers; but it is the doer that moves ahead and makes things happen for him or herself. Sales is never a job, nor should it ever be regarded as one. It is a career; and the difference between a job and career is about 20 hours a week. There isn't a magic formula for attaining success; you get out of your career exactly what you put into it. I knew a company director who really had a pearl of wisdom: 'The harder I work, the luckier I get'. Or we can say that success is only a matter of luck – ask any failure.

If you feel that your job is taking you nowhere, it is probably time for a change. Fatigue and monotony are the effects of frustration, rather than the causes of it. The right sales position can cure the malady because in the professional field there are few activities as exciting. Sales is, and always will be, the front-line in the war for corporate profits.

In order to be truly effective, salespeople must make no mistake about their loyalties – they must be with the company that they work for. If they don't believe in their company, they can't believe in their product. If they don't believe in their product, they will never be able to sell it effectively. It is imperative to keep goals in line with those of the employer. When they drift apart, you no longer have the anchor to keep the ship moored and prevent it from floundering.

We all have a lifetime contract with the organizations that we work for, and it is renewable every day. We have to strive to improve and learn to accept constructive criticism from people who are there to help. As Ralph Emerson once said: 'Our chief want in life is somebody who will make us do what we can.'

You are now equipped to be as successful *as you personally desire* in your sales career. Arts and crafts can live forever if they are passed on. Helping other people may be your most successful achievement.

THE PROMISE

Vince Lombardi once said: 'You must be willing to pay the price to win. You must be willing to pay the price to stay on top, but most of all you must be willing to pay the price to get there. And the price is hard work.'

Winners aren't born; they are developed. It takes years to become an overnight success. Nobody ever mastered any skill except through intensive, persistent and intelligent hard work. Today's experience is important, but it is no guarantee that it will still be effective tomorrow. Only the principle endures, not the technique. Selling skills must be practised and revised regularly if you are going to keep them sharp.

At the beginning of this book, I promised to give you ten words which, if followed, will absolutely, positively guarantee your total domination over your competitors. They are: ALWAYS GIVE YOUR CUSTOMER A LITTLE MORE THAN THEY EXPECT. These simple words, with their straightforward meaning, can have the greatest single impact on ensuring your future success.

Do you ever wonder how a professional makes what he or she is doing look so easy? It looks easy because it has been practised so much that it becomes reflexive. Professionals do their jobs well, even when they don't feel up to it. Why? Because they work hard at what they do and they don't look upon failures as something too difficult to overcome. They view failures as personal challenges and opportunities to improve. They also give a little more than what's expected of them.

There is no failure except in giving up. It isn't important what you know about your job; it is important what you do about it. The difference between ordinary and extraordinary is just a little 'extra'.

Index